Copyright © 2020 by Pauline W.

All rights reserved. No part of this book may be reproduced or used in any manner without w ... ight owner except for the use of ... For more inform

info@paulin

FIRST EDITION

Last updated in January 2023

www.paulinaontheroad.com

ABOUT THE AUTHOR

Hey there, I am Paulina, writer behind paulinaontheroad.com. I am a fervent travellette with a passion for the great outdoors and sustainable travel.

My love for Cape Verde started in 2016, when I visited the country for the first time. At that time my blog was the only travel resource about Cape Verde in English.

Since then, I keep returning. After visiting almost every island, I share with you the Cabo Verde that you can't find in average tourist guides.

Enjoy the read and don't forget to share with me your favorite places in Cabo Verde.

TABLE OF CONTENTS

5

THE ULTIMATE CAPE VERDE TRAVEL GUIDE

HOW TO ENJOY CAPE VERDE LIKE A LOCAL INCLUDING SUSTAINABLE TRAVEL TIPS, HIDDEN GEMS AND MUST-DO'S ON ANY CAPE VERDE TRIP

1. INTRODUCTION

Hey! My name's Paulina and I am a fervent traveler to the Cape Verdean islands. After traveling to Cape Verde for three times and spending more than half a year on the archipelago, it was time for me to put my passion for this country into a book.

So far, I have been publishing tons of content on my website, paulinaontheroad.com about Cape Verde However, there were several reasons to put all my knowledge of Cape Verde into an e-book.

First, I wanted to gather my travel tips of each Cape Verdean Island altogether and not in loose, separate articles. In this travel guide, you will find exclusive tips that I have gathered onsite and content that I did not publish on my blog.

Secondly, there is no any other dedicated travel guide about Cape Verde in English!

Finally, I wanted to provide a benefit to those who decide to support my research and travel to Cape Verde. That means; you, dear reader! Already now; thanks a million!

You are doing a valuable contribution! With the purchase of this e-book, you are not only helping me, but also the local, small independent businesses of Cape Verde.

Indeed, the focus of this travel guide lays on sustainable travel to Cape Verde. I have spent several months in doing research about small and hidden shops, restaurants and hotels. Thus, you will not find many of the recommended places here in any other travel guide! They are a direct result of my research on each Cape Verdean Island and my passion about the Cape Verdean culture and small businesses.

However, you may wonder why it even matters to put such emphasis on local, small businesses in Cape Verde.

In the last years, the Cape Verdean islands have been undergoing a huge increase in tourism! Sal and Boa Vista have been turned into massive tourist hubs in less than ten years! Whereas this is a great development for the national economy, one should not lose out of sight the side effects of this evolution!

It is striking how most of the new businesses related to tourism are created or managed by foreign companies or expats! No matter where you go, you will find out that foreigners manage the most popular restaurants, hotels or shops! While there is nothing bad about this, it is crucial that the local community has a share of this massive growth too.

You might ask yourself why don't the Cape Verdeans simply copy the strategy of foreign companies and create successful travel businesses by themselves.

This is a question that I have discussed with tons of locals and expats, and there is not one correct answer! Some of the explanations can be found in the colonial past and the isolation of each island. However, one thing is crystal-clear; the Cape Verdean businesses lack the funds of large, international companies and the skills when it comes to online marketing.

That is where this travel guide comes in! I wanted to put the small, independent and local businesses into the spotlight. After my trips to Cape Verde, I have noticed how many restaurants, hotels and shops lack a Facebook page and are not present on TripAdvisor or Booking. In addition, even if you are in a city like Nova Sintra (Brava) or Porto Ingles (Maio), it is hard to find the local restaurants or hotels as they are often hidden away in secluded streets.

This does not mean that you cannot find the most renowned tourism businesses in this guide! In addition, it does not mean that if you stay in a large resort, you are necessarily a bad person! I just wanted to lay the focus on the fact that behind the shiny façade of tourism in Cape Verde, there is so much more to be explored, and that with your purchase; you can make a real impact and contribute to a positive change!

Thus, already now, I want to thank you for your support and decision to make the benefits of tourism enjoyable to the local community.

Please note that this document contains affiliate links. That means if you purchase via them, I'll earn a small commission. At no extra cost for you. They help me to maintain the site. Thanks a lot already.

I really hope that you will enjoy this guide as I have put my heart and soul into it. I am also very open to hear your feedback, ideas or latest discoveries from the Cape Verdean islands. Feel free to drop me a message to *info(a)paulinaontheroad.com.*

2. GENERAL TIPS

2.1.   BEST TIME TO VISIT CAPE VERDE

The Cape Verdean islands are a year-round destination because they have a subtropical climate. The average annual temperature ranges between 26°C and 30°C.

The best time to travel to Cape Verde is from September to February. It is then when the temperatures are still not too hot. It is thus perfect for a winter sun getaway too!

If you are planning to do hiking holidays, I recommend visiting between August and October. That is when the rain season leaves the islands of Santo Antao, Fogo and Brava in a lush green, even phosphorene color! The rain season in Cape Verde cannot be compared to the rain season in Asia. Often, the rain is very sparse. Thus, you will still be able to go hiking.

January is the perfect month to experience the mountainous islands of Fogo, Santo Antao and Sao Nicolau.

Visit Mindelo (Sao Vicente) in February as it hosts one of the most important carnivals. There are daily events during the carnival season. Percussion and dance groups start rehearsing in early December.

The autumn and spring months are dry with very little rainfall, making them the best time to go to Cape Verde for sunny and dry weather.

As of 2020, the last three years, the country has been suffering of a lack of rain. That is why Cape Verde is considered being one of the most affected countries by the climate change.

2.2. VISA

A visa to Cape Verde can be purchased on arrival at the airport at a cost of 25 €. This tourism visa must be used within 60 days of its issuance. It allows its holder a stay of 90 days, which can be extended for a maximum of an equal period.

2.3. HOW TO GET AROUND

Once you have figured out how to get around in Cape Verde, it is very easy to move around the different islands.

Flights:

The islands with international airports are Sal, Boa Vista, Sao Vicente and Praia.

The islands with national airports are Maio, Fogo and Sao Nicolau.

In order to move between the islands by flight, I recommend Skyscanner and check for flights with BestFly Airlines. The flight schedules are reliable unless you fly to Maio.

Ferries:

If you are traveling on a budget and want to mingle with the locals, I recommend the inter-island ferries.

Me personally, I do not have a particular preference for the boat or a flight. It really depends on the time that I have at my disposal. Please also note that sometimes, the sea can be really though. Thus, I recommend always taking anti-seasickness pills with you!

The islands that can <u>only</u> be reached by ferry are Brava and Santo Antao.

The schedules and tickets for ferries between the islands can be found at cvinterilhas.cv

Car Rental:

Until recently, car hire in Cabo Verde was one of the most complicated things to do as a foreign visitor. Luckily this changed and you can now find numerous car rental deals via caboverdecarhire.com.

They partner with local car rental companies from Cabo Verde.

2.4. MONEY AND COSTS

The currency of Cape Verde is the *escudo* (100 Esc = +/- 0,91 €)

I always travel with my Wise card as it saves me tons of fees! I never had an issue paying bills with it.

I recommend getting your money from an ATM. Each international airport in Cape Verde has one. You can take out a maximum of 20.000 Esc (+/- 181,45 €) with a fee of +/- 165 Esc (+/- 1,50 €).

Credit cards are only accepted in larger and medium-size businesses. That is why I always recommend taking cash with you! Some businesses charge an extra fee of 200 Esc (+/- 1,81 €) when you pay with a credit card! Thus, please, always make sure to ask in advance!

The costs of traveling to Cape Verde strongly depend on the island that you are visiting.

If you travel to Sal or Boa Vista, you can expect prices such as in Central Europe. As everything has to be imported, the prices are extremely high and barely unpayable for the local community.

If you travel to the "hiking islands" such as Fogo, Brava or Santo Antao, you can estimate 30 € per night + 25 € in food per day. These are average amounts and of course, there are always cheaper or more expensive alternatives!

National flights can quickly cost 100 € per journey and ferry rides vary between 20 and 50 €, depending on the island that you plan to visit.

2.5. SAFETY

First, I want to state that I have never had any bad experience in Cape Verde when it comes to security matters! I had one dubious encounter in Mindelo at night but luckily, I managed to get rid of this shady person.

I have heard and still hear many warnings about the security situation at night in the outskirts of Praia, Mindelo and recently in Sal.

When in Praia or Mindelo, please stick to the main tourist areas and be cautious at night!

When in Sal or Boa Vista, be cautious when walking back to your hotel at night! I have heard from some expats that they only travel by taxi at night. Also, please keep an eye on your belongings! Sal and Boa Vista used to be both very quiet and safe places. However, with the arrival of tourism, the easy money and the luxury that they cannot afford are attracting shady persons.

In my eyes, the safest islands in Cape Verde are Maio, Brava, Santo Antao and Sao Nicolau.

2.6. HEALTH CARE

During my travels in Cape Verde, I just had to stay in a hospital once and I have to admit that I was very surprised by the quality! This was in Mindelo. Unfortunately, the health care services depend a lot on the island that you are visiting.

If you get seriously sick or injured when being in Maio, Fogo or Brava, you will most likely have to travel to Praia to visit a proper hospital. Such events can rapidly explode your travel budget, as you need to be transferred to another island.

That is why I strongly recommend getting a reliable health and travel insurance!

I got mine with HeyMondo. It is extremely easy to set up, reliable and has an online support via its app. On top, it is very affordable. In one word, it is fabulous!

2.7. SIM CARDS AND INTERNET

If you want to stay connected with your beloved ones at home, I recommend purchasing a SIM card upon your arrival at the airport. Indeed, depending on the island you are visiting, you will not always find Wi-Fi in restaurants or hotels.

You will find two stands: one by *Unitel* and one by *CVMovel*. I always opt for *CVMovel* as it has the best network on the remote islands.

You can get 8 GB for 12 €.

2.8. VEGETARIAN AND VEGAN FOOD

The options for vegetarians and vegans vary a lot from island to island. If you are in one of the greener or larger islands such as Santo Antao, Sao Vicente or Santiago, you will have more vegetarian/vegan options.

If you are staying in Sal or Boa Vista, the food will be European and international. Thus, you will not have any problems when it comes to veggie alternatives.

However, things tend to become a bit more complicated when you travel to the smaller and dryer islands such as Maio, Fogo or Sao Nicolau. The food supplies are depending on the boats that come from the other islands. On top, the veggies are often excessively boiled. Especially in Maio, I had to pay attention to get all my proteins and vitamins!

As a general tip, I recommend buying your own fruits and vegetables, and eat them as a raw snack between your meals.

3. OVERVIEW – MAIN HIGHLIGHTS OF EACH ISLAND

In terms of beach holidays, Maio, Sal and Boa Vista are the best options. However, that does not mean that you should ignore the other archipelago gems! Indeed, some hide a paradise for hikers, such as Santo Antao, or dramatic volcanic landscapes, such as Fogo.

Whereas Sal and Boa Vista are the most touristy islands, it is absolutely worth it to go beyond and explore the colorful, rich culture and landscapes of the other Cape Verdean islands!

After visiting each island of the archipelago, I want to share with you a non-exhaustive list of the best things to do in Cape Verde and the most gorgeous attractions in Cape Verde.

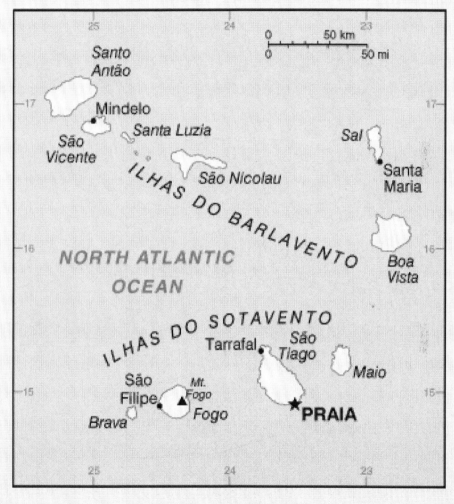

Map of Cape Verde

3.1.   SAL ISLAND

USEFUL INFORMATION

How to get there:

By plane: to Sal International Airport

How to get around:

By taxi or by *aluguer* (collective taxi)

Where to stay:

Hilton Cabo Verde Sal Resort *****

Oasis Salinas Sea *****

Melia Dunas Beach Resort & Spa *****

Hotel Budha Beach *****

3.1.1. VISIT SANTA MARIA AND ITS BEACH

Santa Maria is the main tourist hub of Sal. Most of the resorts, hotels, restaurants and bars are located here. The town is famous for its beach that boasts turquoise water and extremely fine sand.

There are many bars and restaurants on the beach, which will serve you the finest fish.

The highlight of Santa Maria Beach is the pier where the locals sell their fish. It is the best place to watch the daily grind and interact with the locals.

3.1.2. HEAD TO KITE BEACH

Kite Beach is only a 10 min drive away from Santa Maria. It is one of the best beaches in Cape Verde for kitesurfing! It is very windy and the waves are extremely strong!

Even if you do not kitesurf, you can just relax at the bar and watch the stunts of the surfers.

If you are eager to learn, there is a kite school on site. You can borrow material or get a kitesurfing lesson.

3.1.3. VISIT THE BLUE EYE - BURACONA LAGOON

Visiting the *Blue Eye* is probably one of the most popular tours from Santa Maria. Also known as, "*Buracona*", this place has a very special, almost magical atmosphere.

The lagoon is located northwest of the island and a perfect place for a swim.

If the sunrays hit the water, its color turns turquoise and allows you to see the ground of the water.

3.1.4. VISIT THE PEDRO LUME SALT MINES

Sal is small and mostly desert. Besides the *Buracona* lagoon, the salt mines of Pedro Luma are a must-do.

Located in the east of the country, they can be visited with a guided tour or by *aluguer* (collective taxi).

If you reach the village, you can already feel the remote vibe. To me, it felt like a ship graveyard, as there were plenty of them. There is also the emblematic church that makes a great photo motive.

Once you actually make it to the salt mines, you will stand in front of a natural wonder that once made Sal one of the wealthiest islands of Cape Verde!

Tourists can float in the salty waters of the salt mines and learn more about the salt production back in time.

There is also an excellent restaurant next to the mine's entrance. It serves some of the best fish carpaccio I have ever eaten in my entire life!

3.1.5. GO TURTLE WATCHING

Did you know that Cape Verde has the third-largest population of nesting loggerhead turtles in the world?

If you love animals, turtle watching is essential! Particularly on Sal, Maio and Boa Vista.

Indeed, the archipelago is one of the most important places in the world for turtle nesting! The best time to spot turtles is between July and October. However, please, always book a tour with a professional guide and respect the turtles!

3.1.6. GO DIVING

If you love to dive into the big blue, I recommend that you go diving. Whereas there are also dive clubs in Boa Vista and Maio, you have the largest offer in Sal.

3.2.   BOA VISTA

How to get there:

By plane: to Boa Vista International Airport

By ferry: to Sal Rei port

How to get around:

By taxi or by aluguer (collective taxi)

Where to stay:

Terra Kriola

Iberostar Club Boa Vista *****

Hotel Riu Karamboa ****

Hotel Riu Palace ****

Hotel Riu Touareg ****

24

3.2.1. DO WATERSPORTS

Boa Vista is one of the best places to do water sports. Not only is the water extremely clear but on top, there seems to be a beach for every taste.

Whether you just want to have a relaxing swim, watch turtles or get active, there is a beach for you!

When it comes to watersports, you can opt between kitesurfing, windsurfing, surfing, sailing, kayaking or diving. As you see, you will be spoilt for choice if you enjoy being in the sea!

3.2.2. VISIT THE VIANA DESERT

The Viana Desert is one of the natural wonders of Cape Verde! Located in the northwestern part of the island, it is one of the top things to do in Cape Verde!

On a stretch of 5 km, the Atlantic winds carried the fine sands of the Sahara to Boa Vista. It is a place where you will wonder at nature and its tranquility!

In order to visit the desert, you should book a tour, and please note that access to motor vehicles is limited!

3.2.3. EXPLORE SAL REI

Sal Rei is the capital of Boa Vista and with its 6.000 inhabitants, it's almost home to more than half of Boa Vista's population!

However, it is not a bustling capital. Sal Rei is famous for its relaxing and laid-back vibe. If you love colorful architecture, the colorful houses and churches will amaze you!

Praca Santa Isabel is the heart of Sal Rei and here, you can purchase souvenirs and local food. The church of *Igreja da Santa Isabel* is probably one of the prettiest attractions of Boa Vista.

I also recommend taking the time to sit down at a bar, have a local drink and just soak up the Cape Verdean vibe of "No Stress!"

3.2.4. VISIT THE SHIPWRECK ON CABO SANTA MARIA

The massive shipwreck on Cabo de Santa Maria Beach quickly became one of the most popular attractions of Cape Verde. It is probably the most popular photo motive of Boa Vista!

Standing out tall of the water, the remains are from a large cargo ship that ran aground in 1968 while crossing the Atlantic.

Today, the shipwreck is a source of inspiration for local artists and a popular destination for tours from Boa Vista. It is one of the prettiest things to do on Cape Verde.

Please note that recently, petty theft has raised on Cabo de Santa Maria Beach!

3.2.5. RELAX AT CHAVES BEACH

Chaves Beach is located in the western part of the island. This 5 km long beach is probably one of the best beaches in Cape Verde!

The gold-white sand is extremely fine and you will be amazed by the saturated turquoise color of the ocean! There are almost no facilities, but it is a great place for a swim. If you are lucky, there will be some wind so that you can even go windsurfing!

During July and August, Chaves Beach is one of the best places to go turtle watching in Cape Verde. However, please remain respectful and keep your distance!

How to get there:

By plane: from Praia to Fogo National Airport

By ferry: to Fogo

How to get around:

By taxi or by *aluguer* (collective taxi): departing near the market

Where to stay:

The Colonial Guest House

Pipi's Guest House

In the volcano crater (a must do!):

casa alcindo

Casa Marisa

Where to eat:

Tropical Club Bar

7Sois7Luas - Espaço 24

Pipi's Bar

3.3.1. CLIMB THE VOLCANO

Mount Fogo is probably one of the most stunning natural attractions of Cape Verde! No wonder that it is considered one of the seven natural wonders of the archipelago!

If you are a nature lover and prefer to explore Cape Verde's highlights by slow travel, climbing Mount Fogo is essential, as it is one of the main attractions in Cape Verde.

The hike takes around five hours and is of moderate difficulty. You will go up to 2.829 m! You can also opt to do the *Pico pequeno* (small volcano).

The trail starts in Cha das Caldeiras and I recommend asking your host to organize a guided hike. Indeed, the trail is not easy to find and it can even be dangerous to climb the volcano!

I recommend staying at *Casa Alcindo* as he is not only an extraordinary guide, but also provides beautiful accommodation inside the crater!

Guided tour the big volcano: 40 € approx.

3.3.2. DO A WINE TASTING

Did you ever associate wine to Cape Verde? Well, Fogo is home to the only wine production on the entire archipelago!

The grapes are growing inside the crater, which gives the wine of Fogo its unique, characteristic taste. Fogo's wine is only selectively exported. Thus, you will taste a true gem!

The entire production is eco-friendly and managed by small, local and family-owned businesses.

In order to visit the wine cellars, follow the signs after reaching the crater.

3.3.3. BUY LOCAL COFFEE

Fogo boasts the largest coffee production in Cape Verde. The plantations are all located in the surroundings of Mostreiros and can be visited.

However, you do not need to head to Fogo to purchase coffee from Cape Verde. Almost each supermarket on any island sells the tasty coffee beans. Just ask the vendor for *kriola* or *emicela* coffee.

3.3.4. VISIT THE COLONIAL TOWN OF SAO FILIPE

There are only a few towns in Cape Verde that can compete with Sao Filipe from an architectural perspective!

The bright, colorful buildings, the town's grid layout and the cobblestone paved narrow streets are symbolical for colonial architecture.

Most hotels are located in Sao Filipe and I recommend staying at least one night in order to dive into the local, easy-going grind. A walk at night in Sao Filipe is one of the most scenic experiences in Cape Verde!

3.3.5. HIKE FROM CHÃ DAS CALDEIRAS TO MOSTREIROS

If you think that hiking up the Mount Fogo volcano would be the only hike to do on Fogo, you could not be more wrong!

There is another spectacular trail from Cha das Caldeiras to Mostreiros waiting for you!

It could not be more contrastful to the bare, deep-black sands of the volcano! You will cross a lush-green eucalyptus forest, and come across coffee and banana plantations. You will wonder how farmers can climb up the extremely steep hills to cultivate potatoes, peas and papayas!

I particularly liked the extremely saturated green colors of Mother Nature. They seemed even brighter after experiencing the baren, black sands of the volcano crater.

The hike takes around five hrs and is of intermediate level. Ask your host in Cha das Caldeiras to bring your luggage to Mostreiros.

A taxi from Mostreiros to Sao Filipe costs 6.000 Esc (+/- 54,45 €).

3.3.6. ENJOY LOCAL MUSIC

Before Cape Verde became a coveted holiday destination, the archipelago was mostly known for one thing: its music! *Cesaria Evora* exported the most famous music genre of Cape Verde: *morna*.

However, there are plenty of talented musicians excelling at *morna*. If you want to enjoy the local music and support the local artists, I recommend attending a concert at the *7Sois7Luas* in Sao Filipe.

The center is the cultural hub of the island and is home to an excellent restaurant. A must thing to do on Fogo!

3.4.   SAO VICENTE

How to get there:

. By plane: from Europe and Praia to Sao Vicente International Airport

By ferry: from Praia and Sal -cvinterilhas.cv

How to get around:

By taxi or by *aluguer* (collective taxi): departing from Praca d'Estrela

Where to stay:

Hotel Foya Branca

Pont d'Agua Hotel ***

Aquiles Eco Hotel

OASIS Porto Grande

Casa Branca ****

Where to eat:

Elvis Restobar (Mindelo)

Le Gout de Grills (Mindelo)

Fundo d'Mar (Mindelo)

Marina (Mindelo)

Cantinho da Brasa – Churrasqueiro (Mindelo)

Chez Loutcha (Calhau)

Hamburg Bar (Calhau)

3.4.1. ENJOY THE CULTURAL SCENE OF MINDELO

Mindelo is also known for being the cultural capital of Cape Verde. Not only is it the hometown of *Cesaria Evora* (the most famous Cape Verdean singer!), but it also boasts numerous museums and art shops.

The variety and cultural wealth of Mindelo is partly due to its marina and harbor. For a long time, the port was the main gate for exports and imports. Nowadays, Mindelo is home to the only marina in Cape Verde. There is thus always a large international community.

To me, one of the best places to enjoy the cultural wealth of Mindelo is *Nho Djunga Library*. It hosts concerts on a regular basis in a very hip, relaxed location.

3.4.2. VISIT THE MINDELO MARKET

One of my favorite places in Mindelo is definitely the covered market. In fact, there are two markets in Mindelo. The first one is the most traditional and ancient one.

It is located in *Rua de Libertad d'Africa* street. The building alone is worth a visit!

The second one is open air and located on Praça d'Estrela. Here, you can get all kind of fruits, vegetables, electronic gadgets and clothes.

My highlight was the tailors from the African mainland who will make you a tailor-made dress within three days!

It is definitely one of the best souvenirs to get in Mindelo!

If you are brave enough, head to the fish market. Located next to the small replica of the *Torre de Belem*, it is definitely the smelliest place of Mindelo!

However, those who dare to visit will be rewarded with an authentic experience and learn more about the variety of the fishes that Cape Verde has to offer.

3.4.3.   HIKE MONTE VERDE

Even though Sao Vicente is often seen as a gate to Santo Antao (a real paradise for hikers!), you can also do nice hikes in Sao Vicente.

One of the best ones is without any doubt climbing Monte Verde. It will provide you with breathtaking views over Mindelo, Monte Cara and neighboring Santo Antao.

In order to get to the trail, take an *aluguer* (collective taxi) to Calheta and ask the driver to drop you off at the feet of Monte Verde.

The hike is of intermediate difficulty and takes about 2-3 hrs.

3.4.4.   DINE OUT IN CALHAO

I probably had the best meal of all Cape Verde in Calhao! The small town is a coveted destination for Sunday excursions, which consist in eating all day long!

There are two main restaurants in Calhao: *Hamburgo* and *Chez Loutcha*. Both are competing for the title of the best fish and seafood barbecue in Cape Verde!

If you want to enjoy the legendary buffet of *Chez Loutcha*, book your experience ahead. in Chez Loutcha hotel in Mindelo. Prices include transfer to Calhao.

Restaurant Hamburg is much smaller but the grilled baby squids were some of the best that I ever had in my entire life!

If you want to extend your visit, head to Calhao Beach, which is one of the prettiest of Sao Vicente.

3.4.5. WINDSURF IN SAO PEDRO

Somehow, Sao Vicente holds something for each type of traveller. Also, for water sport lovers!

If you come with your own material, you will find great surfing conditions in Salamansa Bay or Baia das Gatas.

However, the best conditions for wind surf can be found in Sao Pedro. It is a scenic bay and there are several companies where you can rent your surfing gear.

If you do not want to get wet, I recommend hiking to the lighthouse *Farol da D. Amalia*. It provides some of the best panorama views on the island!

3.4.6. EAT A CACHUPA

You cannot leave Cape Verde without tasting its *cachupa*! It is the most typical food from the archipelago.

Each restaurant and family have his or her very own recipe and you can have *cachupa* on each island.

It consists of corn and beans, topped with a fried egg. To make it extra tasty, a slice of fried *linguiça* (sausage) is added. *Cachupa* is one of the cheapest foods to eat in Cape Verde.

I particularly liked the *cachupas* in Mindelo and my favorite one was the one at *Dokas*. Set in a cool, rather sophisticated location with perfect Wi-Fi, you can get a *cachupa* for 1,5 €! Add a fresh fruit juice to it and you will have the perfect foodie experience in Cape Verde!

3.5.   SAO NICOLAU

How to get there:

By flight: to Sao Nicolau National Airport

By ferry: from Santiago (Praia) and Sao Vicente (Mindelo)

How to get around:

By taxi or by *aluguer* (collective taxi): only until 6 pm!

Where to stay:

Bed & breakfast Regina

Zena Star

Edificio Magico

Casa Patio

Where to eat:

- *Didi Evora Restaurant*
- *Restaurante Bar Didi Evora*
- *Bar Felicidade*
- *Ka So Pizza*

3.5.1. VISIT CARBEIRINHO

The rock formations of Carbeinho are considered as one of the seven natural wonders of Cape Verde!

If you are visiting Sao Nicolau, it is essential on each visit to marvel at Mother Nature's artistry!

The rock formations and shapes will remind you of the Grand Canyon! Just that in Sao Nicolau, you can have a refreshing swim next to the rock formations!

3.5.2. HIKE MONTE GORDO

Monte Gordo, a magnificent mountain volcanic in origin, rises to 1.312 m, the highest point on Sao Nicolau.

It is the perfect place for those who enjoy hiking in remote places.

Indeed, tourism is not very developed in Sao Nicolau. Thus, you will get a unique privileged experience!

3.6.   SANTO ANTAO

How to get there:

By plane: from Europe and Praia to Sao Vicente International Airport

By ferry: from Sao Vicente to Santo Antao

How to get around:

By taxi or by *aluguer* (collective taxi)

Where to stay:

Casa Santa Barbara Deluxe

Ribeira Grande Country House

Biosfera Amor do Dia

Tiduca Hotel

Lombo Branco Village

Where to eat:

Casa Maracuja

Cantinho de Amizade

Artesanato Divin'Art

Cantinho do Gato Preto

3.6.1. HIKE THE COVA CRATER - PAUL VALLEY TRAIL

Santo Antao is famous for being a paradise for hikers. There are countless trails awaiting you and one is more scenic than the other one. In total, I stayed more than ten days in Santo Antao and I found it too short to do all the hikes that I wanted to do!

Thus, even if you are staying only two days in Santo Antao, I recommend doing at least the most scenic trail: from the Cova crater through Paul valley.

Take an *aluguer* (collective taxi) to Cova and have a quick breakfast at *Biosfera do Amor* that offers splendid views over Sao Vicente. Their handmade jams and bread are a real delight!

Hike down the crater until the trail takes you up to the crater's borders. From here, you will enjoy the best view of Santo Antao.

The entire trail goes downwards and lasts about three hrs. You will pass through scenic villages where you can stop at a local bar and have a drink or traditional meal.

3.6.2. ENJOY THE STREET ART OF RIBEIRA GRANDE

Santo Antao is not all about nature! If you want to enjoy local street art and culture, I strongly recommend heading to Ribeira Grande. Have a walk through the city and explore its colorful murals.

Even though the town might appear to be grey at first sight, the colorful street art will make your city walks much more enjoyable.

If you cannot get enough of the local, contemporary art, head to the *7Sois7Luas* center. It hosts concerts and exhibitions on a regular basis. It is definitely one of the best places to get to know the local artists.

3.6.3. TAKE A DIP IN THE NATURAL SWIMMING POOLS

Unfortunately, Santo Antao does not boast many beaches (except Tarrafal on the southern side). The few beaches that you may come across may seem tempting, but please keep in mind that it is extremely dangerous to swim here!

Thus, in order to be on the safe side when it comes to swimming, take an *aluguer* (collective taxi) to Sinagoga (15 min from Ribeira

Grande). This quaint village boasts some of the best natural swimming pools in Santo Antao.

They are completely safe. Ask the locals for the *"piscinas naturais"* (natural swimming pools) or head directly towards the ruins on top of the rocks.

3.6.4. VISIT FONTAINHAS, THE PRETTIEST VILLAGE OF CAPE VERDE

Some consider Fontainhas as one of the natural wonders of Cape Verde. No wonder when you know that even National Geographic awarded the label of "prettiest village of Cape Verde" to the scenic setting of this small village!

It is definitely a must-do when visiting Santo Antao! I recommend discovering the village by foot. It is an easy hike away from Ponta do Sol and lasts about one hour.

When in Fontainhas, make sure to enter the village and have a drink at *Tchu's Bar*. His fruit juices are a real delight!

3.6.5. HAVE A GROGUE AND LOCAL FRUIT

Santo Antao is also known as being the garden of Cape Verde. The fruits and vegetables coming from Santo Antao are sustaining almost ⅓ of the entire archipelago's population.

One of the lushest valleys is probably Paul valley. It is home to countless coconut, papaya, banana and mango trees.

Thus, when in Santo Antao, ask at the restaurant for the season fruit and indulge in coconut biscuits, passion fruit *caipirinhas* and banana breads.

Santo Antao is also home to one of the largest *grogue* production sites on the archipelago. The local *schnapps* is made of sugar cane and used to prepare tasty *caipirinhas*. If you want to go for the softer option, try a *ponche*. It's a liquor prepared with local fruits such as passion fruit, coconut or tamarind.

3.6.6.   HIKE UNTIL YOU DROP

If you enjoy hiking, Santo Antao will be your heaven! After staying for more than 10 days on Santo Antao, I did not have enough time to do all the hikes I wanted!

The volcanic landscape created plenty of valleys, and each of them has a different microclimate. Some trails take you to villages such as Corvo or Fontainhas that seem to be cut of from time.

So far, not many trails are indicated. However, there are efforts to put landmarks in order to help the hikers. In most cases, the trails are former *caminhos vecinais* (vecinal paths) that were used to interconnect the villages.

Some of the best hikes on Santo Antao are:

- Cova crater - Paul valley
- Ponta do Sol - Cha d'Igreja
- Montetrigo – Tarrafal de Montetrigo
- Ribeira Grande - Xoxo
- Corda - Coculi

3.7. SANTIAGO

How to get there:

By plane: from the USA, Southern America and Europe to Praia International Airport

By ferry: from most islands

How to get around:

By taxi or by *aluguer* (collective taxi): departing from *Sucupiro Market*

Where to stay:

Pestana Tropico

King Fisher Village

OASIS Praiamar

Kama Ku Kafé – Pousada and B&B

3.7.1. VISIT CIDADE VELHA

Santiago is home to Cidade Velha, declared "Intangible Heritage of Humanity" by the UNESCO! It is the first city to be built by the Europeans in the South of the Sahara and it was the capital of Cape Verde until 1770.

The original design of the settlement is still intact and you will feel like you dived right into the 16th century! It is impressive how the original features remained untouched!

Cidade Velha was one of the most important places for the Atlantic trade of enslaved persons. That is why it is also considered as one of the birthplaces of the first developed Creole societies.

3.7.2. EXPLORE THE BUSTLING CAPITAL

Praia is a "love at second sight affair". Before visiting, I mostly heard that it was a dangerous place, for locals and tourists alike. Then, when you arrive, you will spot countless grey, often unfinished houses or resorts.

However, Praia's magic becomes evident after you scratch on the surface.

The main tourist area is the *Plateau* where you can enjoy the administrative buildings in colonial architecture style. Do not forget to visit the market, which is considered one of the prettiest in Cape Verde!

From here, head towards Prainha and Quebra Canela to enjoy a drink at the numerous beach bars that recently opened.

3.7.3. HAVE A MUSIC NIGHT OUT IN PRAIA

If you are interested in enjoying the Cape Verde's rich musical culture, Praia is the place to be! *Quintal da Musica - 5al da Musica* hosts live concerts in Cape Verde's most famous music styles such as *morna, funanana* and *coldeira.*

Some of the best music bars in Praia are:

- *Fogo d'Afric Restaurante/Bar & Club*
- *Quintal da Musica – 5al da Musica*
- *Kebra Kabana*

The music festivals that you should not miss:

- *Kriol Jazz Festival*
- *Festival Gamboa*
- *Virada d'Anu*
- *Noite Branca*

3.7.4. ENJOY THE BEACH OF TARRAFAL

Tarrafal Beach, located in the north of Santiago, is often considered as one of the prettiest beaches in Cape Verde!

Indeed, it is different from the beaches of Maio or Boa Vista, as Tarrafal Beach has palm trees and a very laid-back, surfer vibe that you cannot find on any other island. On top, it has white, fine sand and the only coconut trees of the southern islands.

There are plenty of accommodation options and restaurants. Thus, I recommend staying at least a few days in order to enjoy the "No stress!" vibe.

3.7.5. HIKE IN SERRA DA MALAGUETA

Santiago holds something for any type of traveler. It is not only an island with an immense cultural offer, but also with numerous hiking trails for nature lovers.

The best hikes of Santiago can be found in Serra da Malagueta. With a total surface of 774 hectares and 25 endemic species, the natural park is one of the most important parks of the archipelago.

There are hikes for any level, whether you are up to a two hrs hike or an eight hrs one!

You can reach the entrance gate of Serra da Malagueta by *aluguer* (collective taxi) from Praia, Assomada and Tarrafal. Just tell the driver that he should drop you off at Serra da Malagueta.

Entrance fee to the natural park: 200 Esc (+/- 1,81 €)

3.7.6. VISIT THE MARKET OF ASSOMADA

The market of Assomada is the most important market of Santiago. It is even livelier than the market of Praia!

Whereas every day is "market day" in Assomada, Tuesdays and Saturdays are the most important days. On these days, the market duplicates in size!

From early in the morning until 5 pm, you can buy anything from vegetables and fruits, to souvenirs, fashion and even animals!

Visiting the market of Assomada is definitely a unique way to dive into the Cape Verdean daily grind.

3.8. MAIO

How to get there:

By ferry or by flight: from Praia, Santiago

How to get around:

By taxi or by *aluguer* (collective taxi): departing from Praca Publica, only until 6 pm!

Where to stay:

Barracudamaio

CASA EVORA.COM

Villa Maris Ecolodge

Stella Maris Villa

A great way to enjoy Maio like a local, is by renting a holiday home. On top, they are quite affordable!

Where to eat:

Restaurante 7Sois7Luas (best view in town!)

Tropical Bar Restaurante

Big Game

Bar Tibau

Restaurante Xaxa

Restaurante Agencia Cortina

3.8.1. CHILL AT THE BEST BEACHES

To me, Maio has the best beaches in Cape Verde! Whereas the "beach islands" such as Boa Vista and Sal have stunning beaches too, they became victims of large tourist resorts and mass tourism during the last years.

Maio seems to be a precious gem that managed to protect its still pristine beaches and unspoiled character. On some beaches, you can literally walk for hours without ever crossing a soul!

That being said; do not expect many facilities! The beaches of Maio are still in their original state.

Some of the best beaches in Maio can be found close to the capital, Vila do Maio. In order to explore the other ones, I recommend taking a taxi or renting a bike.

Some of the best beaches in Maio are

- Bitche Rocha
- Ponta Preta
- Beaches of Ribeira Dom Joao (for surfing!)

- Praia de Santana

To me, it is definitely the best place to go in Cape Verde for pristine beaches.

3.8.2. EAT FRESH GOAT CHEESE

Fresh goat cheese is one of the star products of Maio. Almost each household produces its own. It is in Ribeira Dom Joao that one of the first goat cheese factories was built.

Maintained exclusively by women and supported by the European Union, I strongly recommend visiting them and supporting this small, local business.

They have also installed a little bar where you can taste their freshly made goat cheese.

Address: Main Road of Ribeira Dom João, ask for "*Senhora Rosalina*".

3.8.3. ENJOY A PRIVATE CONCERT WITH CAPE VERDEAN MUSIC

If the gross domestic product of Cape Verde could be measured in terms of music, the country would clearly be one of the richest in the world!

Whereas *Cesaria Evora* and *Mayra Andrade* are Cape Verde's most famous exports, there are plenty of local artists to be discovered! You will hear some of the songs during your entire stay, as music is simply everywhere in Cape Verde!

If you want to support local artists in Cape Verde and have a VIP experience, why would you not organize a private concert? The cultural centers of *7Sois7Luas* are fostering and supporting local musicians. They are spread out throughout the archipelago and at any of them; you can order a private music session.

Find all the information and contacts at 7sois7luas.com or at *Restaurant 7Sois7Luas* in Vila do Maio.

3.8.4. GO TURTLE SPOTTING

Did you know that the flattest island in Cape Verde is also one of the most important places for turtle nesting? In fact, the extensive sandy beaches of Maio are important for the nesting *Caretta Caretta* (loggerhead turtles), second only to Boa Vista.

In order to preserve this unique wealth, the *Maio Biodiversity Foundation* was created in 2010, with the main objective to know and protect nature for sustainable development. For this purpose, the foundation invites, both national and international volunteers, to come to Maio for an extended stay and support their endeavours.

If you are only staying for a short time in Maio, ask for a turtle nesting tour at the office of the *Maio Biodiversity Foundation* pink building at the church square.

3.9.   BRAVA

How to get there:

By ferry: from Fogo

How to get around:

By taxi or by *aluguer* (collective taxi): only until 6 pm!

Where to stay:

Hotel Pousada Nova Sintra–Brava

Hotel Djabraba's Eco-Lodge

Hotel Cruz Grande Brava ***

Residensia Ka Denxu

Where to eat:

Bar Mansa (Nova Sintra)

Djabraba Eco-Lodge (Nova Sintra)

O Castelo (Nova Sintra)

Restaurante Paulo (Nova Sintra)

Por-do-Sol (Faja d'Agua)

3.9.1. EXPLORE THE COLONIAL TOWN OF NOVA SINTRA

Nova Sintra is the only island capital that is not located on the sea. After arriving in Furna with the ferry, a long winding road takes you up to Nova Sintra, with its 1.500 inhabitants.

Named after the Portuguese town near Lisbon, Nova Sintra shares some characteristics with its Portuguese equivalent. It has a humid and fresh climate, surrounded by lush greenery and fabulous views on the ocean.

Even the floors and the houses have been built in an architectural style that remembers Portugal. In my humble opinion, Nova Sintra is one of the prettiest cities in Cape Verde!

3.9.2. SWIM IN THE NATURAL SWIMMING POOLS OF FAJA D'AGUA

After Nova Sintra, the bay of Fajã d'Agua is a must-see on Brava. Cut out on an imposing escarpment dotted with colorful hues, Fajã d'Agua is a place to watch time go by.

However, the natural swimming pools of Fajã d'Agua are the real attraction of the village. With its crystal-clear waters, it invites its visitors to have a refreshing bath. For me, the swimming pools are some of the best Cape Verde tourist attractions.

Fajã d'Agua can be reached by hiking or by *aluguer* (collective taxi).

3.9.3. HIKE, HIKE, HIKE!

Brava has plenty of trails to be explored! Serving initially to connect villages, they are nowadays mostly used by tourists that fell in love with Brava's rough landscape.

Also known as *"Ilhas das Flores"* (Island of flowers), your hikes will be a green delight if you visit between August-October. Colorful bougainvillea, hibiscus and jasmine flowers frame the trails.

Hiking Trails on Brava:

- Mato Grande: I recommend hiking up to Mato Grande to have a priviledged view on Fogo and its massive volcano.
- Fontainhas trail: 4 hrs, start at the Mira Beleza viewpoint
- Hiking to Fajã d'Agua

3.9.4. ENJOY SOME OF THE BEST CAPE VERDEAN MUSIC

The rhythm of Brava is easy going and Nova Sintra has an almost enchanting, relaxing atmosphere.

In order to mingle with the locals and to get to know the music of Brava, I recommend watching out for the small *tocatines* (traditional music halls) in the bars or even in the private houses that are open to visitors.

I am a big fan of the *7Sois7Luas* band of Brava. *Rosa*, the main singer, is "a power of nature", as friends of mine call her! Her charism and the rythm of the band are unbeatable! You will fall in love with the Cape Verdean music!

Ask at the *7Sois7Luas* center in Nova Sintra about their next performances.

4. IN-DEPTH GUIDES: THE BEACH ISLANDS

4.1.   SAL

Sal became in less than ten years one of the most important tourist destinations in Cape Verde. If you visit today, it is hard to imagine how pristine and tranquil the beaches of Santa Maria must have been.

Nowadays, there are plenty of beach clubs, discos and resorts. As a result, it might be difficult to get a sense of the real Cape Verdean culture. Because, after all, you will be enjoying the same travel experience as if you would travel to Southern Spain or Greece.

That is why I strongly recommend planning an island-hopping trip to any of the surrounding islands. Thanks to the airport, Sal is very well connected and it is easy to get around.

If you do not have the time to visit other islands, spend a day in Espargos or Palmeira to live the Cape Verdean daily grind and support local businesses.

4.1.1. USEFUL INFORMATION ABOUT SAL

How to get there:

By plane: To Sal International Airport and by taxi or *aluguer* (collective taxi) to Santa Maria.

Where to stay:

Whereas Palmeira is the capital of Sal, Santa Maria, in the southern part of the island, is the main hub. Most hotels, activities, and restaurants are located here.

Budget

Pontao Hotel ***

Hotel MiraBela (Les Alizés)

Sakaroule B&B

Aparthotel Santa Maria Beach

Mid-Range

The Budha Beach Hotel ****

Odjo d'Agua Hotel ****

Agua Hotels Sal Vila Verde ****

Hotel Morabeza ****

Luxury

Hilton Cabo Verde Sal Resort *****

Oasis Salinas Sea *****

Melia Dunas Beach Resort & Spa *****

Hotel Budha Beach *****

Melia Llana Beach Resort & Spa *****

Melia Tortuga Beach Resort & Spa *****

4.1.2. BEST THINGS TO DO IN SAL

4.1.2.1. HANG OUT AT SANTA MARIA

Santa María, the end station of Sal's main road, is a bubbly and colorful village and on the way to becoming a major tourist destination. Big hotels are in construction and tour operators increase their volumes every season.

Prices are high, comparable to northern Europe.

The fantastic, sandy beach with turquoise water, and its perfect conditions for kitesurfing, are its main attractions.

Nevertheless, you can still see at any corner, tracks of the African-Creole atmosphere like at the *Mercado Municipal* where you can buy local fruits and crafts.

Please, visit the tailor from Senegal. It´s a true artist! I could not resist ordering him a tailor-made dress with cloth from Guinea-

Bissau. In a few hours, he tailors you any model from your favorite fashion magazine!

4.1.2.2. ROAD TRIP FROM PALMEIRA TO SANTA MARIA

Palmeira is the first harbor for sailors coming from the Canary Islands.

It takes you +/- 40 min to get from Palmeira to Santa María. Take an *aluguer* (collective taxi) to Espargos (0,50 €) and then another one to Santa María (1 €).

Indeed, it is a fun ride to enjoy the wind breeze in your hair and watch the desert landscape of Santa Maria. I had quite an adventurous feeling.

If you are looking for authentic things to do, a road trip by *aluguer* (collective taxi) or a guided tour is definitely essential!

4.1.2.3. VISIT PALMEIRA

By boat, I arrived in Palmeira, home to the main port of Sal. With the size of a fishing village, you can easily visit the main spots in a few hours.

Palmeira is for me the best place in Sal in order to enjoy a little of the famous, relaxing Cape Verdean vibe. Did you know that the national mantra is "No Stress"! Well, here you can live it first-hand in the numerous bars and restaurants.

Afterwards, I realized that Palmeira is, with Espargos, the most authentic city of Sal. Santa María, in the south, is on the best way to become a tourist stronghold. What I liked most about Palmeira was its colorful house front, which transmitted an almost Caribbean feeling.

Furthermore, prices were half as high as in Santa María!

4.1.2.4. VISIT THE PEDRA LUME SALT MINES

Sal's major attraction is, guess what? The salt mines! You easily get there by any island tour from Santa Maria (+/- 25 €) or by *aluguer* (collective taxi) to Espargos and by taxi to Pedra-de-Lume. This place seems to be a personified ghost town. A place where ships come to die.

The "village" has gone from the richest place on the island to an almost godforsaken spot. 100 years ago, the salt mines gave the island international fame until they became unprofitable.

Nowadays, you visit them for five €. I loved the sensation of floating in the salty water. Even when you are standing on both feet, you are still not sinking! The mud will get you a baby skin again, and all my skin blemishes just vanished!

For me, the *salinas* (salt mines) of Pedra Lume are definitely a must-do when visiting Sal!

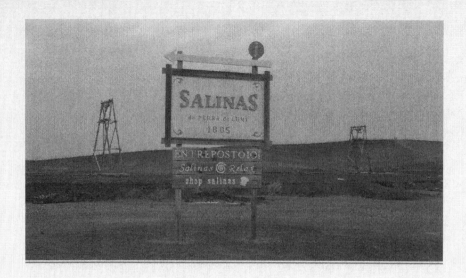

4.1.2.5. VISIT ESPARGOS

In Espargos, you will imbibe the authentic Cape Verdean life. Take your time for a coffee and popcorn on the main square, and watch life passing by. Indeed, most locals do not live in Santa Maria, but in Espargos or Palmeira.

The administrative capital has the most important viewpoint of the island: a hill obscured with satellites controlled by the US, and from which you can oversee the entire island (220 km^2!).

4.1.2.6. TAKE A TURTLE NESTING TOUR

Did you know that Cape Verde is recognized as the third most important nesting area for the loggerhead sea turtle in the world?

Between May and October, you will have the opportunity to assist the *Caretta Caretta* turtles nesting and laying their eggs, as well as baby turtles hatching and making it for the sea.

The activity is carried out at night and you should always keep your distance to the turtles! Be a respectful traveler and listen to your guide!

Keep in mind that it is forbidden to go to the hatching areas on your own! However, you can go with a guide. Some of the beaches are even closed during the breeding season.

4.1.2.7. ENJOY SANTA MARIA BEACH

The beach of Santa Maria is one of the main reasons why travelers visit Sal. Indeed, the sand is golden and very fine. The turquoise colored water will remind you of the Caribbean. It is just the perfect place to relax.

There are several bars and restaurants where you can enjoy a drink or a meal with a sea view.

Sal boasts a few beaches, but the one at Santa Maria is definitely the most famous and most beautiful one!

4.1.2.8. TAKE A KITE LESSON

The second beach of Sal, also very close to Santa Maria is known as "Kite Beach". You can reach it either by *aluguer* (collective taxi) or by walking 20 min from the center of Santa Maria.

From far away, you will already spot dozens of colorful kites.

Sal is a hub for kitesurfers and hosts several championships throughout the year.

You can easily book a kitesurfing lesson or rent some equipment at "Kite Beach".

4.1.2.9. GO SCUBA DIVING

Sal is a great place to go scuba diving because the waters surrounding the island are home to a vivid underwater life. Whether it will be your first time doing a scuba dive or if you are already a half-pro, you will love the experience!

Some of the animals that you will see are for example turtles, pufferfish and little sharks (which do not do anything though!). If you are super lucky, you will even spot some whales!

Please remember to be respectful when you do a scuba immersion! Do not take anything out from the sea, excepted memories!

4.1.2.10. DO AN ISLAND TOUR BY CAR

One of the best ways to explore Sal is by renting a car in Santa Maria and just explore the island on your own. This way of traveling is particularly fabulous for those who are more adventurous and do not necessarily want to follow a guide.

An island tour with a rental car can be done in half a day. However, if you really want to enjoy the local vibe and get to know the local grind, I recommend taking your time and spread out the tour throughout the day.

Please note that you should not drive off-road as you might risk being stuck and destroy the local (sparse!) vegetation.

4.1.2.11. GO SNORKELING

You always wanted to get started with snorkeling. Alternatively, you already have plenty of experience when it comes to snorkeling.

Your vacation might be the perfect moment to do a snorkel tour in Santa Maria. The underwater fauna is extremely colorful and intriguing. It is definitely one of the best things to do in Sal!

The good thing about snorkeling is that you can always come on the surface again. That is why I often prefer snorkeling to scuba diving.

4.1.3.12. ENJOY CAPE VERDEAN FOOD IN SAL

During your trip, you cannot miss indulging in local food.

Of course, there are plenty of international options such as pizza, burgers and ice cream. However, I recommend making the most of your stay and explore the beautiful Cape Verdean hospitality and tasty gastronomy.

The most famous dish is without any doubt *cachupa*. It is a slow cooked stew of hominy and beans with fish or meat. Sometimes, they even add a fried egg or a *linguiça* (local sausage) on top. Each home and restaurant have his or her own recipe.

Some of the best restaurants in Santa Maria are:

- *Sabores Livros Bar/Restaurante*
- *CapeFruit*
- *Cam's — Mercearia Gourmet*
- *Restaurante Barracuda*

4.1.3.13. GO SHOPPING IN SANTA MARIA

My favourite place to shop in Sal is the local market.

Here, you cannot only find plenty of fruits and vegetables, but also many local, artisan shops. My favorite one is definitely the atelier of a Senegalese tailor. I got myself an African-themed dress and it was ready in less than two days!

It is definitely one of the best souvenirs from Cape Verde that I could think of!

I love to approach the street stalls with local fruits or sweets run by African women. You never know what they hold for you. Some even sell delicious sweets with coconut and brown sugar. Yummy!

In November, it is the high season on papaya and bananas.

In addition, here, prices are comparable to northern Europe!

4.1.3.14. DO A SAILING TOUR

To me, sailing is some of the most relaxing ways to travel and on top; it is one of the most sustainable ways to travel as well!

Another advantage of going on a sailing tour around Sal is that you will get to know fellow travelers and that you will enjoy different views on the coast of the island.

Most of the boat tours include the hotel pick up, drinks and even lunch.

4.1.3.15. VISIT "BLUE EYE" LAGOON

The *Blue Eye* also known as the *Buracona* lagoon in the north of the island is one of the highlights of every Sal round tour.

Included in almost every day tour, the lagoon is considered one of the top things to do in Cape Verde. The entrance fee is 6€ but swimming here is a delight!

However, what makes the *Buracona* lagoon so special? It is the magic of the light! Indeed, this beautiful underwater cave turns magic blue and turquoise by the sunlight!

4.1.3.16. GO FOR A SHORT HIKE

Sal is not really the best Cape Verdean Island for hiking. You might be better off visiting Santo Antao, Fogo or Brava.

However, if you are a hiking lover and you absolutely want to explore the island on foot, I recommend hiking to the *Serra Negra* nature reserve.

Located next to Murdreira, this nature reserve is the highest point of Sal with 104 m. You can find the area between Ponta da Fragata in the south and Ponta do Morrinho Vermelho in the north.

The natural reserve is considered as an important site for birdwatching.

Going on a tour with a local expert is the best way to explore the hidden and secret places to see in Sal. I love exploring new places with a guide as you get to know so much more about a place.

Because behind the shiny resorts and fancy bars of Santa Maria, there lays the beautiful creole culture that is absolutely worth exploring.

On top, a local guide will easily provide you insightful answers about the Cape Verdean language, history and culture.

Boa Vista, literally meaning "beautiful view", is certainly a place that does justice to its name. However, where is Boa Vista, and what to do there?

The easternmost island of the archipelago and third largest one awaits visitors who want to experience the authentic Cape Verdean lifestyle.

Slow paces, deserts of sand and scree, low mountain ranges, and miles of amazing beaches, bathed by turquoise waters are just some of the reasons to visit this place. The easiest way to get here is by plane as the airport has operated direct international flights to Boa Vista from all over the world since 2007.

Among the many things to do in Boa Vista, we can mention sunbathing, snorkeling and diving, as well as hiking and safari excursions.

4.2.1. USEFUL INFORMATION

How to get around:

The best way to get around in Boa Vista is by private taxi or by *aluguer* (collective taxi). Most of them depart from the main square in Sal Rei.

Where to stay:

Budget

  Casa Sara Boavista

  Ca Madeira Deluxe

  B&B Salinas Boa Vista

Mid-range

  B&B Sereia Azul Boa Vista

  Cala da Lua apartments

Family-friendly

  Hotel Riu Karamboa ****
  Cala da Lua apartments
  Ouril Hotel Agueda ***

Something different

  Terra Kriola

Luxury

Iberostar Club Boa Vista *****
Hotel Riu Karamboa ****
Hotel Riu Touareg ****

4.2.2. THINGS TO DO IN BOA VISTA

1. EXPLORE SAL REI

Sal Rei, Boa Vista's capital, is a cozy, sleepy town counting slightly over 6.000 inhabitants. Undeniably, the town's most famous landmark is the *Igreja da Santa Isabel*, a colonial-style church overlooking the square with the same name.

The baroque facade, painted in shades of sand and royal blue, merges perfectly into the colorful landscape of the square, characterized by flowers and pavilions.

Sal Rei got its name from the saline near the town, where only the best quality salt was produced.

Other highlights of this small colonial town are the harbor, as well as the colorful districts that impress with their little houses aligned along the streets.

Do not miss the market where you can stock up on local fruits and vegetables.

2. VISIT THE SHIPWRECK OF THE CABO SANTA MARIA

Undeniably, one of the best excursions in Boa Vista is to head to Praia de Santa Maria in order to admire the iconic shipwreck of the *Cabo Santa Maria*. Beached in 1968 while sailing towards Brazil, the today's rusting wreck provides one of the most photogenic landscapes on the island!

A place to visit if you are eager to get that "Insta-worthy" shot! On top, it is one of the most important attractions in Cape Verde!

3. ENJOY THE MUSIC BARS OF SAL REI

Boa Vista may be much more tranquil than Sal, but the island still offers plenty of entertainment opportunities. One of the best things to do is to enjoy music in one of the many bars in Sal Rei.

Nestled near the harbor, the super-cozy *Wakan Bar* is renowned for its vibe, friendly staff and awesome cocktails. Not only can you listen to music here, but also the bar actually hosts live events regularly.

The Cocoa *Bar* is another nice place with a great atmosphere and good music. If you are looking for something less crowded, you could go to the *Cabana Tropical Bar & Grill*. It is one of the best things to do in Boa Vista.

4. EAT TRADITIONAL CAPE VERDEAN FOOD

Cape Verde is known for its delicious food that blends a West African heritage with Portuguese influences.

So, what is some traditional Cape Verdean food you should try? Seafood is exquisite in Boa Vista! You can choose from many local dishes, including shrimp in a garlic and wine sauce, *moréia* eel (served fried), laps, stew made from mussels and peppers, or lobster cooked in a red sauce.

One of the best places to taste all these specialties is the *Beramar Restaurant*, a fusion cuisine restaurant run by a talented Milanese chef, and near the waterfront close to Sal Rei Plaza.

Despite its Italian origins, the chef knows just how to respect the local dishes, and uses only freshly sourced ingredients.

Another great place to eat is *Fado Crioula*, a place that serves delicious food all day long and cocktails in the evening. If you are bored, you can even join one of their jam sessions or other cultural events that they regularly organize.

5. RELAX ON PRAIA DE CHAVES

Many claim that Praia de Chaves is one of the best beaches in Cape Verde! Flanked by the fanciest hotels, this white sand beach impresses with its azure waters and wonderful dunes.

The beach includes all modern amenities, from sunbeds and umbrellas to showers and toilets. It is also famous for having some of the best hotels in Cape Verde.

In addition, if you were after an affordable five-star experience, why would you not book your stay at the *Iberostar Club Boa Vista*?

This All-Inclusive seafront resort not only has great rooms with ocean view, but it also offers a wide range of services, from a seafront pool to a bar, spa treatments, an on-site night club, as well as room service.

6. ENJOY A LONELY WALK AT PRAIA DE SANTA MONICA

While Praia de Chaves could be crowded sometimes, Praia de Santa Monica, in the southwestern part of the island, is perfect for a lovely afternoon stroll.

It is about 5 km away from Povoação Velha, a splendid colonial village and only 16 km from Sal Rei.

Adjacent to the Morro de Areia nature reserve, the beach is also the perfect spot for observing the local fauna. If you are lucky, you might even spot some sea turtles!

7. VISIT THE VIANA DESERT

Opposite to Praia de Santa Monica, in the northwestern part of the island, the Viana Desert is a place like no other! You can get here easily from Sal Rei or Rabil to admire the ever-changing landscape made up of white sand dunes.

Interspersed with sparse vegetation and black volcanic rocks, the dunes create a surreal landscape!

The unearthly feel is amplified by the lack of any artificial sounds. No doubt, this is the place to visit to restore your energy or meditate!

What makes it even better is that the desert is located at only a stone's throw from civilization. You will not have to worry about deadly animals or quicksands, and walking here is absolute bliss!

8. EXPLORE THE RABIL OASIS

Unlike Sal, which is quite sandy, Boa Vista impresses with a few green places. Such as the Rabil oasis. Stretching along the river Rabil, the oasis offers a different kind of landscape.

The terrain is quite arid, but you will be able to admire lots of palm trees, as well as other desert vegetation.

Perhaps the loveliest spot around the mouth of the river is the wetland, an important natural area.

The Rabil lagoon is home to many species of birds, including the Eurasian spoonbill and rufous-backed sparrow. Birds apart, you can also spot indigenous lizards, like the Cape Verdean leaf-toed gecko.

9. EXPLORE THE DESERTED VILLAGE OF CURRAL VELHO

Have you ever dreamed of exploring a deserted village? You can tick it off your bucket list! Curral Velho was once a flourishing fishermen village, but due to its remote location at the end of Praia de Santa Monica, the settlement was too exposed to pirate raids.

Slowly, as the rest of Boa Vista's settlements started to build fortifications to ward off unwanted attacks, the inhabitants of Curral Velho started to abandon their homes and move to safer areas.

Eventually, the village was completely abandoned, but the ruins of the settlement are still standing proof of its existence.

Not only visiting this place will allow you to discover a bit of the most authentic Boa Vista, but the village is also home now to birds and sea turtles, who come here to lay their eggs.

10. WATCH THE WINDSURFERS AT PRAIA DE VARANDINHA

On the southwest coast of the island, Praia de Varandinha is a windsurfer's paradise!

The crystalline waves bathing the shores, as well as the constant winds, create the perfect surfing conditions.

Surfing apart, the beach itself is a true marvel! Almost deserted, it impresses with amazing caves and coves, as well as the finest sands that are a real pleasure to walk on.

Close to the Morro de Areia nature reserve, the beach is also the perfect starting point for a hiking excursion.

11. GO DIVING OR SNORKELING

Maybe you have always dreamt of snorkeling or diving but never had a chance to practice it.

Figuring in the top ten hotspots for diving and snorkeling in the world, Boa Vista stands out with an impressive diversity of its corals and marine animals.

An abundant population of sea turtles makes it possible to admire these beautiful creatures, both onshore and under the water. Snorkeling tours are possible at high tide in the shallower waters of the reef.

Expect to encounter thousands of colorful fish, as well as some sharks, which are relatively small and not dangerous to humans.

Diving enthusiasts can practice both freediving and scuba diving to explore the amazing sea bottom.

Whatever your choice, please remember to always go with a mate as the ocean can be a dangerous environment!

12. LEARN A NEW WATERSPORT

The best thing that you can do during your holidays in Boa Vista is learning a new watersport.

It could be windsurfing or water skiing. Whatever your choice, many resorts and schools' welcome tourists to join their classes. *SeaBookings*, for instance, offers beginner kitesurf courses, and organizes water excursions by kayak and boat tours.

If you are not sure what sport to learn or what school is best, ask your hotel to book the classes for you with a trusted provider.

13. GO ON A TURTLE NESTING TOUR

Cape Verde is the world's third reserve for the *Caretta Caretta* (Loggerhead) sea turtles, and most of these wonderful creatures deposit their eggs on the beaches in Boa Vista. Therefore, if you happen to visit between July and mid-October, you could embark on a turtle nesting tour.

Who knows; maybe that you will even be lucky enough to see a few youngsters hatching!

81

While many tour operators include this touching experience in their holiday packages, the best thing to do is contact the *Turtle Foundation* in order to find out about the most sustainable ways to observe sea turtles in their habitat, and without disturbing their nesting and hatching.

14. DO A QUAD TOUR

Are you looking for a different experience? An island tour by quad will undeniably be the best part of your stay!

One of the best companies to check out is *Quad Zone*. Established by local individuals, it offers a variety of tours, including a full day tour that will take you to the discovery of the island's best-kept secrets.

If you do not want to go on an organized tour but still like the idea of exploring the island by quad, know that, they also offer quad and scooter rentals to the enthusiasts.

15. GO WHALE WATCHING

Have you ever dreamt of a close encounter with humpback whales?

These friendly creatures come to Cape Verde to give birth, normally in spring. Therefore, if you are planning a trip between March and May, a whale-watching boat tour could be the experience of your lifetime!

Tours depart from most of the hotels and include a short briefing and half an hour of navigation before being able to observe the whales in the company of a marine biologist.

16. VISIT THE LIGHTHOUSE OF MORRO NEGRO

Seeing Boa Vista from above is another of those unmissable experiences to live while visiting the island!

In addition, one of the best places to go for this endeavor is the Morro Negro, a hill located on the east coast of the island. Overlooking the surroundings from 156 m, the Morro Negro lighthouse is a true landmark.

Built in colonial style in 1930, the now-abandoned edifice stands 12 m tall and impresses with its beauty.

Easily accessible from Cabeça dos Tarrafes, the Morro Negro hill is also the access gateway to one of the largest turtle nature reserves on the island.

17. DO A SAILING TOUR

One of the most luxurious experiences to live, and affordable enough for anyone to do, is a sailing tour around the island.

You can pick from a variety of options, including family boat tours, perfect for the youngsters, as well as romantic tours for couples.

This relaxing getaway not only give you a chance to restore your energy levels, but you will also be able to admire the island from afar, and discover some of the prettiest spots along the ever-changing coastline.

If you feel like it, you can even ask the skipper to drop the anchor and freshen up with some swimming or snorkeling. No doubt, an adventure like no other!

18. HAVE A COCKTAIL NIGHT IN A BEACH BAR

After a long day of sailing, diving or exploring the island on a quad, you will certainly need a fun night. Sipping cocktails in a beach bar is by far the best you can do, and there are dozens of interesting bars.

From all, the *Boavista Social Club* impresses the most with its authentic atmosphere given by the wooden decor and straw umbrellas.

The *Blu Mery* might be a restaurant, but the facility has a bar too and prepares delicious cocktails. *Caffè Del Porto*, overlooking the old port in Sal Rei, not only offers yummy cocktails and authentic cuisine, but also organizes live music nights.

19. ENJOY CAPE VERDEAN TRADITIONAL DRINKS

Undeniably, the only way to end your holiday is with a sip of the traditional beverage; *grogue*. Similar to the popular rhum up to some extent, *grogue* is an alcoholic beverage made from sugarcane.

This beverage is also the base for the popular Cape Verdean cocktail *ponche*, which includes lime and molasses. Despite being a bit on the sweet side, it is as refreshing as a mojito and undoubtedly a great choice after a hot day!

Some cocktail bars even use *grogue* instead of rhum for classic cocktail recipes, such as mojito or caipirinhas. Therefore, you really have quite a few ways to try it. It is one of the most typical drinks from Cape Verde after *grogue* and *ponche*.

And now that you know what to do, how's the weather like, what foods to taste and drinks to sip, what are you waiting for?! Pack your suitcase, board that plane, and get ready to live the travel experience of a lifetime!

4.3.   MAIO

I found paradise! I will provide you the directions but under condition that you do not tell anybody! Because the island is such a gem that it seems unreal to have all those beaches for yourself. All alone.

After Sal and Boa Vista, Maio is Cape Verde's third "beach" island. However, it radically differs from its two beachy, sister islands, as it achieved to keep its original charm and keeps fighting to preserve its virgin beaches from aggressive, multinational investors.

Maio has been under threat to end up the same way as Sal and Boa Vista: massive hotel resorts, unsustainable management of resources, inhuman working conditions for the local community and massification of its golden, sandy beaches.

So far, the main obstacle for tourists to invade the island has been the difficult access to the island. Indeed, there are only a few national flights and a few ferries per week.

On top, the politicians are making a great job when it comes to choosing carefully who can invest on the island and who cannot. They are making great efforts to avoid the same errors and damages that happened in Sal and Boa Vista.

I can guarantee that you will not only fall in love with Maio's landscape but particularly with its warmhearted people and the ultimate relaxing atmosphere.

I felt very privileged to experience the pure beauty of Maio, but I left with the bittersweet sensation that it will only a matter of time until the tourists will invade this small paradise.

How to get there:

By plane: only from Praia (Santiago). Flights to Maio only go 3 times a week and take 15 mins. For international flights to Cape Verde, you might want to check (the often very cheap) flights to Sal or Boa Vista and then take a national flight to Praia.

Check Skyscanner for national flights with BestFly Airlines. From the airport, you need to get an *aluguer* (collective taxi) to Vila do Maio.

By ferry: from Santiago. It is a highly irregular schedule but you can check it with *CVinterilhas.com*. I recommend avoiding the ferry as the sea can be very rough!

Public Transport: *aluguers* (collective taxis) are departing from Vila do Maio (aka Porto Ingles) to all major towns on Maio.

Extra Travel Tip: Ilha do Maio can be easily combined with a visit to Fogo. As of March 2020, Wednesday is the best day to travel from Brava–Fogo-Maio because the trip can be done in one day, before the afternoon you're already in Maio.

Where to stay in Maio Island

Barracudamaio

Casa Evora

Villa Maris Ecolodge

Stella Maris Villa

A great way to enjoy Maio like a local, is by renting a holiday home. On top, they are quite affordable!

Where to eat in Maio Island

- Restaurante 7Sois7Luas (best views in town)
- Tropical Bar Restaurante
- Big Game
- Bar Tibau
- Restaurante Xaxa
- Restaurante Agencia Cortina

Where to book tours: Agencia Cortina or Fundaçao Maio Biodiversidad

4.3.1. BEST THINGS TO DO IN MAIO

4.3.1.1. ENJOY THE BEST BEACHES

I am sorry if I will only speak in superlatives about Maio's beaches. Alternatively, in battered terms of "amazing" or "breathtaking". Because they simply are!

In all my travels, I never came across such vast, but completely deserted beaches. Even the beach of the capital Vila do Maio (or Porto Ingles) was very empty. I could not control myself and just started running around on that beach like a fool! The sensation of being incredibly privileged to enjoy natural beauty in such a pure state was simply too overwhelming!

Despite its limited size, Maio has a large number of beaches. Rocky coasts alternate with golden or even white sandy beaches. Porto Ingles (Maio's capital), has two beaches. Bitche Rocha where the fishermen are arriving and the "Porto Cais" behind the pier where it is very dangerous to swim.

4.3.1.2. RELAX IN VILA DO MAIO (PORTO INGLES)

Vila do Maio, also known as Porto Ingles, is probably the most relaxing capital I have ever been to in my entire life! The largest municipality and capital of Maio, the city has two main axes: Avenida Amilcar Cabral and the main island road leading to Figueira. The city got its name "English Port" from the English shipmen exporting the island's salt.

The colorful houses, turquoise waters and warm-hearted local community create a very relaxing atmosphere. I could only think that I did not want to leave. You can easily spend entire afternoons on a terrace (my favourite one being the one of 7Sois7Luas) and watch the fishermen's daily grind. Needless to say, that sunsets in Vila do Maio are an experience of its own.

Vila do Maio is the ideal departure point to explore the island and its quintessential Cape Verdean towns. I invite you to wander through its colourful streets, explore the municipal market and visit one of the prettiest churches on the archipelago. Several investments have been made to renovate Maio's fortress, Castelo do Maio, and a beautiful beach promenade on Vila do Maio's cliffs has been created.

4.3.1.3. VISIT THE SALT MINES OF PORTO INGLES

For centuries, Maio has been famous for its salt. During the 17th and 18th, English merchants came to buy the island's precious product. Still nowadays, you can visit the salt mines, located at the capital's extremity.

The visit of the salt mines is free and I loved to get an interesting insight in the island's main business. Formerly exported to Brazil and Europe, Maio's salt is nowadays mainly exported to Praia and the sotavento (southern) islands of Cape Verde.

Only women run the cooperative. The contrast between the bright, white conical salt piles against a dark green mountainous backdrop and deep blue sky will stay forever in my mind.

Maio's salt is still harvested in a traditional way, which you could still find in Algarve only a few years ago. That means that the *flor do sal* (salt flower) is still picked by hand. By purchasing salt from Maio, you will thus get an entirely organic and pesticide-free product!

Several funds, mostly from the European Union, have been created to build a museum and to broaden the uses of the salt such as wellness or beauty treatments. The museum hosts a bar and a little shop with local, hand-made souvenirs.

Still in Vila do Maio (or Porto Ingles), you'll have the unique opportunity to enjoy the authentic Cape Verdean music.

For me, music is one of the main riches of the archipelago. *Cesaria Evora* being the most prominent ambassador, Cape Verde has an incredible variety and quantity of local artists. Each island has its peculiar style and bands on its own. Music is a key element of everyday life.

Even though some of the most popular musical forms are *Funaná*, *Coladeira*, *Batuque* and *Cabo love*, *morna* still remains the most prominent one. Lyrics are in Cape Verdean creole and include instruments like *cavaquinho*, clarinet, accordion, violin, piano and guitar. Some songs are deeply melancholic, whereas others are full of joy.

In Maio, you will have the best opportunity to listen to local musicians in a unique setting. The *7Sois7Luas* center, located in a former hospital with the best ocean view, is the local main hub supporting Cape Verdean musicians.

4.3.1.5. DO A LOCAL GASTRONOMY WORKSHOP

The *7Sois7Luas* (the cultural neuralgic center of Maio) also offers the unique opportunity to participate at a cooking workshop. *Su*, the main chef of the center, will be your teacher and she'll give you a valuable insight in the Creole cuisine and tell you a lot about the life on the island.

After the cooking workshop, your meal will taste 3 times better and you will enjoy it with a privileged view on Vila do Maio's main beach. A colorful sunset will make this one of the most unforgettable experiences you can have on Maio.

Feel free to call *Su*, the Chef (+2389594542) to organize your cooking workshop.

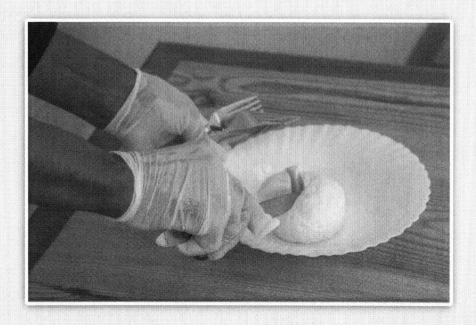

Maio has much more to offer than the sleepy and relaxing vibe of Vila do Maio. A day trip to Ribeira Dom João is the perfect way to explore more of the island's beauty.

Located in the south east of the island at 20 mins. From the capital, Ribeira Dom João will lure you with its colourful house fronts and welcoming atmosphere. The town is also the main hub for cheese production. Did you know that the main economic activity of Maio was goat breeding?

Supported by European funds, a cheese factory with a quaint bar has been built in order to support the local entrepreneurship. Cheese making has a long tradition in Cape Verde and I really enjoyed getting a detailed insight in the process.

It is also the perfect way to get in touch with the local community and learn more about the Cape Verdean culture. It is thus a perfect form of sustainable tourism, as it is all about learning, cultural exchange and interaction.

25-50 cheeses are produced per day and exported to the neighbour islands of Santiago, Sal and Boa Vista. However, the production strongly varies according to the rainfall and the seasons. The goat milk usually takes 24-48 hours to coagulate and only organic and pesticide-free ingredients are used.

Rosalina, one of the main managers, took great care of me and explained the cheese making process with tremendous dedication. Needless to say, that I had a great time and appreciated her warm-hearted kindness!

The cheese factory of Ribeira Dom João is located in the middle of the town's main street. Like the salt mines, 16 women manage the cheese factory.

In case that the factory is closed upon your arrival, ask for *Rosalina Cardoso* or *Damiana*. Do not be shy! Just approach the inhabitants and they will be more than happy to help you!

4.3.1.7. VISIT BARREIRO AND ITS COLOURFUL HOUSES

Do you want to get the "Insta-perfect" picture from Maio? Even though the entire island looks like straight from a travel calendar, you will be particularly spoilt for choice in Barreiro.

Located in the south and only 10-15 min away from Vila do Maio, Barreiro is famous for its colorful housefronts. Indeed, each house is painted in a different color, creating a relaxing vibe around the village.

Barreiro is thus the perfect photo location for your pictures and a lovely place to absorb the sleepy vibe of a small town. You easily get to Barreiro by *aluguer* (collective taxi) from Vila do Maio or by renting a quad.

4.3.1.8. GO TURTLE WATCHING WITH THE MAIO BIODIVERSITY FOUNDATION

Turtle watching is a relatively new activity on the Cape Verdean islands. Indeed, eating turtle meat had been a long tradition on the islands, but a law has prohibited it since 2018.

Many efforts have been made to sensibilize the population. Instead of eating them, the turtles should be preserved and cherished, as they are a great tourist attraction.

By deciding to go on a turtle watching tour with the *Maio Biodiversity Foundation*, you'll on top directly support a local business. The turtle species that you can spot on Maio can only be found here! It is thus very important to fight against their extinction!

During the turtle watching activity, you will assist the nestling of the turtles. The guides from the *Maio Biodiversity Foundation* take great care that the activity is respectful with the animals and that you only spot them from distance.

Once the turtles are laying eggs, spawning, you cannot approach or touch them as they enter in a state of trance.

The turtle watching experience usually takes places at nightfall, when it is dark. Even though it is not a 100% guaranteed that you would spot some, the turtle watching is great fun and I enjoyed waiting with my guide on the beach at night.

Maio Biodiversity Foundation

Pink building behind the church, Assomada Zone, Porto Ingles

ecoguias.maio@gmail.com

4.3.1.9. HIKE MONTE PENOSO AND MONTE BRANCO

Despite of its limited size, the island is very diverse. Along its breathtaking beaches, it also offers several hiking trails and apparently, each season; more and more travellers decide to explore the island by bike.

It is quite flat, thus exploring is a great way to enjoy slow travel on Maio.

Even though Maio is arid, the dry landscapes are contrasted with Acacia forests, palm plantations like in Ribeira Dom Joao even green oases.

Monte Penoso (Mount Painful) is a great hiking destination and day trip from Vila do Maio. With its 400 m height, it is a relatively easy hike, providing a great view on the island. Monte Penoso, the highest point of the island, is located between Alcatraz and Pedro Vaz.

Monte Branco is located right next to Monte Penoso and it is perfect if you want to extend your hike. Together with Monte Penoso, Monte Branco covers a protected landscape of 11 km².

Travel agency: *Contina Viagem* (+2382551218 or +2389874866)

If your time to explore Maio is limited, (even though I recommend taking several days to enjoy it!), I advise to make an island tour and spot Maio's prettiest attractions in one day.

The tour can be done either with a guide, or by renting a quad. In case you opt for the quad, you can arrange rental at the *Big Game Hotel* or the *Maio Info Center*.

As the roads are not the best and the dunes natural park in the north is hard to access, I recommend going by quad or jeep.

My island tour with *Bemvindo* (who has been guiding tourists for 20 years) was great fun and he took me to the most emblematic spots. Thanks to him, I had the chance to discover his favorite beach, Praiona, which is one of the most spectacular, empty beaches that I have ever seen in my entire life!

On your island tour, I recommend to reserve lunch in advance at *Etna's* (a typical restaurant in Calheta, +2389830839). You can also just show up, but be ready to wait some time for your lunch, as it is all freshly prepared. In the meanwhile, I recommend taking a swim on the beach right next to the restaurant.

I suggest the following itinerary for an island round tour:

- Departure in Vila do Maio
- Ponta Preta at the Stella Maris resort
- Barreiro for the colorful house fronts
- Figueira da Horta with its former *grogue* (sugar cane *schnapps*) factory
- Ribeira Dom Joao with its cheese factory and beach
- Alcatraz near Monte Penoso
- Cascabulho close to the dunes natural park
- Calheta for lunch at *Etna's*
- Morro
- Arrival in Vila do Maio

4.3.2. DISCOVER THE BEST BEACHES

If you want beach holidays, Maio has the best beaches on the entire archipelago!

The best beaches in terms of being unspoiled and free of the mass tourism that you can find on Sal or Boa Vista.

In all my travels, I never came across such vast and completely deserted beaches. Even the beach of the capital Vila do Ingles, located behind the pier, was very empty. I could not control myself and just started running there like a fool! The sensation of being incredibly privileged to enjoy natural beauty in such a pure state was simply too overwhelming!

If you visit Maio, I put together this selection of my favorite, unmissable beaches on the island. Some are extremely hard to find, so I hope that this guide will be helpful.

Travel Advice:

The best way to visit the most secluded beaches of Maio is by quad or 4x4 car. You can rent them in Vila do Maio.

Please note that there are no trash bins and no food facilities. That is why, please take care not to leave any trash on the beaches and bring some food with you.

The beaches of Maio are important biodiversity retreats hosting a unique fauna. Please treat nature respectfully.

Some of the best beaches in Maio are:

1. Praia Real, Terras Salgadas

Located close to Ilha Cao, with a gorgeous mountainous backdrop, a very quiet atmosphere and ideal for swimming. The access is not easy, thus I recommend taking a guide like from *Contina agency* (+2382551218 or +2389874866), or by quad.

Located in the north, behind the dune park and behind Cascabulho. Ask the locals fro Praia Real or Bahia Galeao.

2. Praia do Galeao

In the same area, you will arrive at the beaches named Tartarugas and Cais. On the right side, you can see a huge salt pit. Continue on foot towards the north. You will arrive at the beaches of Galeão and Real. You may see the islet named "Laje Branca".

3. Santana Beach

Leave Morrinho towards the northwest. On a bumpy road, you arrive at Santana Beach. It is one of the wildest and hidden beaches on the island, and preferred by the turtles to lay their eggs. Nearby are the beaches of Calhetinha and Pau Seco that are both worth a swim.

4. Ribeira Dom Joao Beaches

Located on the coastline behind Ribeira Dom Joao (famous for its cheese factory). You need to cross the village and ride along with the palm plantation. There are actually two beaches, which are separated by a rock and sheltered by imposing cliffs. Depending on the waves, the larger one is suited for surfing.

5. Ponta Preta

Located close to the more luxurious *Stella Maris Village*, Ponta Preta gives you a breathtaking view on Maio's coastline. Be ready to be overwhelmed by a 2 km stretch of pristine beach.

Please note that this place can be dangerous because of the currents! Make sure to take a hat and sunscreen with you, as there is no shade!

The topping of spending a day in Ponta Preta is having a sundowner cocktail at *Martin's Restaurant*. Their pineapple caipinihas are out of this world!

6. Porto Cais (Vila do Maio)

Despite its limited size, Maio has a large number of beaches. Rocky coasts alternate with golden or even white sandy beaches.

Vila do Ingles, Maio's capital has two beaches. Porto Cais is one of them and starts behind the pier where it is very dangerous to swim! However, the beach is actually perfect for long walks.

It is here where I had a severe case of spontaneous happiness outbreak! I was squeaking of joy and running around like a headless chicken, and nobody could see me, as the beach was very empty. Well, if I would not have talked about it on the blog!

7. Bitche Rocha, Vila do Maio

The second and main beach of the capital. Despite the fact that it is here where all the colorful boats arrive, it is perfect for a refreshing bath and watching the fishermen's daily grind. There are also a few bars on the beach to enjoy the local vibe. I recommend having some Caipirinhas at the *Bar Tropical*.

8. Bahia Da Calheta

Located in Calheta. Even though it cannot compete with the other beaches, I like it for its easy-going atmosphere and having lunch at a typical restaurant (*Etna's*) closeby.

9. Praia Goncalo

This beach is essential on every island tour of Maio! It is difficult to access and it is a bit smaller than the other beaches of the island. Located next to the village of Santo Antonio, this beach will give you the feeling of being out of this world!

However, it boasts an extremely clean, white sand. Whether it is dangerous to swim here or not depends on the currents. Please always be cautious!

10.   Praia do Morro

Praia do Morro can be compared to Ponta Preta, just that it is even more remote and secluded. Indeed, when I visited, I had this 8 km stretch of beaches all for me alone!

Also, here, please note that there are strong currents and that you need to be vigilant!

You can get back to Vila do Maio by foot (1 h walking) or by taxi.

5. IN-DEPTH: THE HIKING ISLANDS

5.1.   SANTO ANTAO

I found paradise! A land full of tropical fruits, coffee and foreign vegetables. With people so easy-going that you think, you have known them forever. A land where hard physical work pays off and nobody will ask you for a handout. In addition, when children approach you, they will not ask for food or escudos but just for a pencil!

This is Santo Antao, the lush green yard and lung of Cape Verde.

How to get there:

There is no airport (anymore) in Santo Antao, which means that you need to pass via Sao Vicente.

Luckily, Sao Vicente boasts an international airport.

Next step is getting by ferry from Mindelo to Porto Novo (Santo Antao). There are three ferries per day. Please inform yourself at the harbor as schedules may vary!

How to get around:

Once you arrive in Porto Novo, hundreds of taxi drivers will wait for you! I recommend taking a step aside and having arranged your transfer already upfront (for example via *Edson* from *Walk Santo Antao*).

You will have three options to get from Porto Novo to the scenic part of Santo Antao (Ribeira Grande or Ponta do Sol):

1. By *aluguer* (collective taxi): go to a van and wait until it is full. It is the cheapest option.
2. By private taxi (coastal road): the quickest way to reach your destination.
3. By private taxi (mountain road): the most expensive option. However, I strongly recommend it! The landscapes are jaw dropping and considered as one of the most spectacular roads in Cape Verde! Cost: +/- 40 €.

Where to stay:

Lombo Branco Village

Biosfera Amor do Dia

casa xoxo

Tiduca Hotel ****

Casa Santa Barbara Deluxe

Where to eat:

Casa Maracuja

Cantinho de Amizade

Artesanato Divin'Art

Cantinho do Gato Preto

5.1.1. WHY SANTO ANTAO IS SO SPECIAL

Santo Antao has a magic on its own. Secluded and isolated during decades, it is famous for the hospitality and friendliness of its people. The hiking trails are out of this world and will leave you speechless more than once!

During the hikes, you will see the hard but simple life of the inhabitants of the island. The intensive agricultural use of the land made them construct terraces in the most isolated and dizzying corners of the mountains.

Throughout the year, nature is very generous: coffee plants and banana, coconut and papaya trees surround most houses, and depending on the season, you will find mangos, avocados and oranges.

Along the trekking trails, I discovered vegetables I have never heard of before: *igname* (yam), *fruta do pão* (breadfruit), *manioc* (cassava), sweet potatoes and a sheer endless pumpkin variety.

Traveling to Santo Antao means reconnecting to nature and to the simplicity of life.

I tend to say that once you go to Santo Antao, you will always go back!

5.1.2. THE BEST HIKING TRAILS

1. Valle de Paul: Cova – Cidade das Pombas

Difficulty: Medium – Duration: est. 6 hrs

If for whatever reason, you choose to do only one hike on Santo Antao, then Valle de Paul is the one! The trail leads you from the Cova crater through the fertile Valle de Paul to Cidade das Pombas.

Get to Cova early in the morning by aluguer (+/- 4 €, departing from Ribeira Grande) and take up forces in *Biosfera Amor do Dia*. An Italian person runs the hostel and they serve breakfast with self-made bread, jam, and natural juices.

Only the views on Neighbor Island Sao Vicente are worth to step in for a bite. The Cova crater is about 10 min away and at the beginning, you will be in the company of some milk cows. The trail leads you out of the lush green crater.

This is the only ascending inclination of the entire hike until you reach the crater's edge. From here, you will have the best and most breathtaking view ever! The immense Paul Valley is at your feet and you can already spot Cidade das Pombas next to the sea.

Now, the dizzying part of the hike begins. This part of the trail is not meant for those who are afraid of heights because it goes down steeply! The trail ends at a larger paved road that leads you through picturesque farmer villages until you reach Pombas.

On your way, you will pass along coffee plants, mango and avocado trees, countless banana plants and coco palms. Most of the island's fruit and vegetables exports come from this valley. It is particularly fertile due to its microclimate.

As a short stopover, I recommend O *Curral* in Cha de João Vaz. An Austrian couple producing their own sugar cane brandies (grogue) and food own the place with ingredients grown in their garden. While you are enjoying a local fruit salad with natural yogurt, you can watch how the workers get the ingredients for today's lunch.

Although the place is a bit pricey, with every bite, you will taste their freshness and *savoir-faire*.

When you keep walking on, papaya and passion fruit trees will surround you. The only direction is downwards. It is impossible to get lost. For those who want to fill up their minibar at home, visit the *grogue* factory in Cidade das Pombas.

If you are looking for a good lunch option in Cidade das Pombas, I recommend *Casa Maracuja*. The restaurant located on a rooftop with gorgeous views to the valley serves fresh seasonal food. Many of their meals are based on passion fruit. You have to try the self-made passion fruit *ponche*! It is delicious!

I loved the restaurant's interior design using passion fruit plants to cover the terrace and the chill-out area. All the furniture is "passion fruit-yellow". However, the heart and soul of this place is *Hetty*, a cheerful woman who seems to speak any language!

After the descend to Paul Valley, I would feel the pain in my knees for several days! It is a strong descend for several hours! However, this trail is definitely worth it! In Cidade das Pombas, you get *aluguers* (collective taxis) to any other larger village on the island.

2. Ponta do Sol – Chã de Igreja

Difficulty: Medium (but very long!) – Duration: est. 6-7 hrs

This hike is one of the most popular ones on the island! It goes along the northeastern coast and passes through villages with no access to paved roads. The views on the valleys and cliffs are some of the most impressive on the island!

This hike is medium difficult. It does not have a lot of increase, but is quite long!

Due to the last raining seasons, the trail has been damaged at some parts. Be prepared that it will be hard to find an *aluguer* (collective taxi) in Chã de Igreja! You may organize your transport in advance or you take one of the taxis from Chã de Igreja back to your hotel.

With some fellow hikers that I met on the trail, I organized myself and shared the costs of a taxi. Many hikers pass the night in Chã de Igreja.

The trail starts in Ponta do Sol, the touristiest village of Santo Antao and a stronghold of French emigrants. For those who do not want to start their hike with an empty stomach, I recommend *Residencial Sintanton Trekking*, which is a hostel specialized on hikers.

On its wall, it has a large map with the most popular treks of the island. Staff will be glad to share their valuable hiking knowledge with you.

The path leads you along the graveyard and further on along pigsties. After one hour, you reach Fontainhas, Cape Verde's most picturesque village! After descending sharp serpentines, you reach Corvo. Here, you have a bar if you want to refresh.

I continued on the trail to Formiguinhas ("little ants"). On my way, I met cobblestone producers and youngsters accompanied by their fully charged donkeys.

I reached Forminguinhas and it is the perfect place to have lunch. You have the choice between *Sonia*'s and *Isabel's* bar. *Sonia*'s bar serves lunch (you better reserve in advance!) and offers very spare rooms as well for those who do not want to continue until Cha de Igreja.

Sonia cooks traditional basic Cape Verdean food and she is such a friendly woman. I just did not want to leave!

Calculate 2-3 hrs from Formiguinhas to Cha de Igreja. Until Formiguinhas, you will have no rest points until Cruzinha (2-hrs walk). Make sure to carry enough water or stock up in Formiguinhas!

The trail leads you in sometimes-dazzling heights to the Aranhas valley. By now, it is abandoned and serves as a pasture ground for the herds of the surrounding villages.

The house ruins give the landscape a very particular atmosphere. The lush green color of the *Aranhas* valley contrasts with the rocky coasts I have been seeing so far.

On the way to Cruzinha (the next village), you will walk along several beaches. Although a bath seems very tempting, you should not even set a foot on them! Tights and drifts are extremely strong and easily underestimated! Every year, tourists become victims of the sea because they did not want to renounce on a refreshing bath!

After one hour, I reached Cruzinha, a small fishermen village with breathtaking views on the coast and the ocean. Cruzinha has a few accommodation options as well.

Just before you reach Cruzinha, drivers will already await you at the end of the trail to offer you their taxi services. Do not hesitate to negotiate in case you do not want to continue walking until Cha de Igreja!

Cha de Igreja is set in a fertile valley and it felt so good to be back among civilization after six hrs of hiking. The center of the village is very well maintained and holds many lovely photo motives.

I loved the relaxing atmosphere of this place. From Cha de Igreja, I got back by *aluguer* (collective taxi) to Ribeira Grande for +/- 25 €. Do not hesitate to ask the driver to stop during the ride, since the valley of Cha de Igreja holds some spectacular views for you!

3. Ribeira Grande – Fontainhas

Difficulty : Easy – Duration: est. 3 hrs

As I was based in Ribeira Grande, I wanted to do a hike that did not include any public transportation. Ribeira Grande is one of the larger villages of Santo Antao and a great starting point to discover the island. It is not as touristy as Ponta do Sol, *aluguers* (collective taxis) are easy to catch and the town has several good restaurant options.

A part of this hike is done on the asphalted road connecting Ribeira Grande to Ponta do Sol. The views on the rocky coast and the valleys are tremendous. Before reaching Ponta do Sol (1h30 from Ribeira Grande), you will pass along a poor settlement of tile makers.

For those who want to recover a bit in Ponta do Sol, I recommend *Residencial Sinanton Trekking*. Using the same trail as at the beginning of the hike from Ponta do Sol to Chã de Igreja, the path goes along the graveyard. After 1h30, you will reach Fontainhas. Due to its unique setting in the mountains above a fertile valley, Fontainhas is a very popular postcard motive.

For many, it is Cape Verde's most picturesque village! In addition, if you want to visit only one village of Santo Antão, then it should be Fontainhas! It is just impressive how the houses are enthroning on the giant cliff! During the rainy season, the waterfalls make the setting even more dramatic!

The best place to forget about time is *Bar Tchu*. The owner makes this a uniquely welcoming place. With his big smile, you will feel at home from the moment you step in. *Tchu* usually serves one daily menu made by ingredients of the surrounding gardens.

I also recommend his self-made fruit juices. Every other ingredient that does not grow in the fertile valley, he gets it from Ribeira Grande. Consequently, several days a week, he walks all the way to Ribeira Grande to get the beers and cokes he serves in his bar! At (too) cheap prices.

4. Corda – Coculi

Difficulty: Difficult – Duration: est. 6-7 hrs

I choose this trail upon the recommendation of a Swiss hiker that I met in my hostel. Although this is a very tough one, I never regretted my choice to hike from Corda to Coculi. The views on the unsettled valleys with the blue ocean as a background will leave you speechless for several moments!

The trail leads you through villages that are not used to see tourists. On the fields, you will see the authentic Cape Verdean life of Santo Antao.

Get an *aluguer* (collective taxi) to Corda (departing from Ribeira Grande). The trail starts at the school of Corda whose inhabitants will be glad to show you the direction. Following the trail, you will walk along the fields of intensive terrace cultivation and small wooden huts. You will see plenty of *guayaba* (guava), papaya, and breadfruit trees.

Following the beaten track, you will all of a sudden be in front of a gorgeous panorama view of the lush green valley. The trail goes along a wall and it is definitely nothing for those who are afraid of heights! Soon, you will catch sight of Coculi, down in the valley.

However, it is still a very long and steel way down! The path descends in sharp serpentines and after 2-3 hrs; I finally reaches the first village: Figueira.

This place is full of sugar cane and papaya trees. There is just one little shop selling water and fruit juices.

I was impressed by the terrace cultivation and how people were not afraid to cultivate their fields or carry heavy baskets in dizzying heights! Finally, I got on a paved road again!

The city has good infrastructures (hospitals, supermarkets, etc.). I had a delicious lunch/dinner at one of the only restaurants in town. In those places, you usually cannot choose from a menu card.

You will eat the *Prato do dia* (daily menu) or nothing! From Coculi, you will get back to Ribeira Grande by *aluguer* (collective taxi) or by foot.

Corda — Coculi was definitely one of the longest hikes I had, but also one of those that marked me the most with its remote villages, sharp serpentines, and plenty of fruit trees. Simply mind-blowing!

5. Ribeira Grande – Xoxo

Difficulty: Easy — Duration: est. 3 hrs

If you are looking for a short hike with great views in a short distance from Ribeira Grande, Xoxo village might be the right one for you. Although my main reason for this hike was the funny name of the village.

By *aluguer* (collective taxi), I got to Xoxo. It is set in the slope and the trail through the village takes about 1-2 hrs until you are on the top.

Xoxo preserved its authentic charm and again, the elder women who carried their heavy baskets on their head impressed me! Alternatively, children carrying gas bottles!

Obviously, the people of Santo Antao are used to steep hillsides. Whereas we foreigners are just watching them out of breath.

From the top of Xoxo village, you will have an amazing view of the valley of Ribeira Grande. The trail goes further upwards, but I decided that I would rather go back. My feet were just hurting too much from my previous hikes.

On the way back, on the right, just after leaving Xoxo, you will pass close to a gorgeous waterfall. It might be dried out during the dry season. As an alternative, you can swim in the natural swimming pools in front of Restaurant Melicia.

If you walk for half an hour more, you will be in front of a lovely tiny restaurant whose terrace has a stunning view on the mountains surrounding Xoxo.

Again, there are no menu options; you will just have the *Prato do dia* (daily menu). It was incredibly delicious and cheap. Again, I was overwhelmed by the kindness of the people of Santo Antao.

In case you want to enjoy the gorgeous surroundings of Xoxo for a longer time, I recommend a stay in the lovely country house *Casa do Planalto*.

From the center of Xoxo, it's still about one hour to get back to Ribeira Grande. Which I did by hitchhiking. My feet just were hurting too much!

6. Ribeira Grande – Sinagoga

Difficulty: Easy – Duration: est. 2 hrs

Santo Antao is not particularly known for its beaches. Tides are very strong and waves often very high! You will be always surrounded by the sea, but you cannot swim in it. Despite hot temperatures. The greater was my joy when I heard about the natural swimming pools in Sinagoga.

As usual, you will get there by *aluguer* (collective taxi) or you can walk along the road connecting Cidade das Pombas with Ribeira Grande. In Sinagoga, you have a few bars and *mercearias* (little shops) where you can stock up on water and snacks.

The name of the village comes from a Jewish community that was expelled from Portugal and found a new home in Santo Antao. Nowadays, you can still see the impressive ruins of the synagogue.

After the Jewish community extinguished, the building was used as a sanatorium to help leprosy patients. Despite the macabre historical background, the ruins are a great photo motive.

The natural swimming pools are a bit hard to find. When you come from Ribeira Grande, you will turn left after a huge rock, following the sign "Beach Bar", before you even enter the village.

If you cannot find the path, ask the locals. They will be more then happy to help you!

The path leads you down towards the ruins of the synagogue and the swimming pools. If you continue on the same path, you will get on a large beach, which is very popular among (experienced!) surfers. Be careful! Here as well, the tides are very strong and will just swallow you!

That is why I just got into the water until my hips and contented myself by watching the surfers. Nevertheless, the views on the cliffs are impressive and the sunset was just amazing. In all, Sinagoga is the perfect place for a "take-it-easy" day.

In Sinagoga, you will find the restaurant *Oasis*. Their octopus is a real delight and on top, the restaurant boasts gorgeous views over the ocean! Certainly, a place to stay longer!

7. Hiking to Monetrigo de Tarrafal – Beach

Tarrafal lies in the South-Eastern part of Santo Antão island. It's much flatter and it boasts some of the best beaches on the island. If not the only ones. The beaches in Tarrafal area are the only ones that can be used without any worries.

But still, here, be aware! The Atlantic Ocean is very powerful!

The beaches of Tarrafal have black sand and are several hundred meters long. It's magical indeed.

The route from Porto Novo to Tarrafal takes approximately 2 h. First, on an asphalt road, then, on a cobbled road and finally, taking a dirt track. It's the most beautiful part of the route, where one can admire a breathtaking landscape.

Along the road, you'll probably meet some shepherds with their goat herds. Thanks to the abundant spring water, a large variety of fruits and vegetables can be cultivated: mango, banana, papaya, bread-fruit, sugar cane, yam, manioc, maize, beans, etc.

It is a perfect place for trekking, swimming, snorkeling, fishing and unwind.

This hike is considered as one of the least known hikes in Santo Antao, thus it's perfect for those who want to get a priviledged insight in the Cape verdean daily grind.

8. Ribeira Grande – Xoxo – Lombo do Pico – Melicia Bar

Level: Medium – 5 hours

I did this hike in October 2020 and absolutely loved it for the absolute highlight: a stunning waterfall!

First you walk from Ribeira Grande to Xoxo (can also be done by colectivo). Once you arrive in Xoxo village, hike up, until you reach a bifurcation of the trails 202 and 203.

One of the trails goes left (coming from Xoxo) and goes to Cova. We follow the right path which brings us up to Lombo do Pico.

From here I went with a guide to find the waterfall. You can ask around in the village for someone to take you. Please ask upfront for the price and if they say they'd do it for free, leave at least a generous tip.

From Lombo do Pico you walk on farmer's trails until you reach a panoramic view of the emblematic Xoxo rock.

From here you continue your walk to the waterfall. It's absolutely stunning and majestic. I didn't make the last 100m to the waterfall, since I am too afraid of heights...argh!!

Following along farmer trails next to fields of manioc, igname, coconut trees, almond trees, papayas, mango trees etc. you walk down to the Bar Melicia, famous for its *calda* (sugar cane juice).

This hike goes up to 700m of altitude and down again.

9. Morrador – Vinha – Fajã de Cima – Chã de Mato – Corda

Level: Difficult – 3-5 hours

This is quite a challenging hike but also one of the most spectacular ones that I've done so far in Santo Antao. Starting just next to Xoxo, from the Bar Melicia it takes you up to 1300m to Chã de Mato.

You'll walk zigzagging paths along abandoned villages, others that have only 5 inhabitants left (Fajã de Cima).

You'll be rewarded with jaw-dropping views into the dazzling depths of Xoxo valley and Ribeira de Torre valley. It's merely incomprehensible how people can create agriculture in this setting.

When arriving in Chã de Mato, I had tears in my eyes. It wasn't an easy hike, it just goes up, up and up. But oh so worth it!

From Chã de Mato you follow the Corda street to Corda. Here, make sure to stop at *Cuzinha de Bento* to enjoy their legendary Dutch apple tart along of a self-roasted coffee. The managing couple is the sweetest!

From here you can walk down to Povoação (2h) or hitchhike a car.

10. Cidade das Pombas – Boca de Figueiral – Antenna – O Curral – Lombinho – Cidade das Pombas

Difficulty: Advanced – Duration: est. 5-6 hrs

This is a great hike to do if you've already trekked the Cova-Paul trail. Indeed, this trail will allow to explore Paul Valley off the beaten track and will provide you with some truly breath-taking views.

That said, you shouldn't do the hike if you're too afraid of heights and not without wearing proper hiking boots. I did this hike in trekking sandals and regretted not bringing my sturdy shoes.

The hike starts in Cidade das Pombas and from here to hike up to Boca de Figueiral, a small village. From here you follow a *caminho vecinal* on the left, don't follow the main route. If in doubt, just ask the locals.

From here you'll climb up to 700m and the agricultural terraces as getting more spectacular with every step. You'll pass along some really remote villages, often just consisting of a few houses.

There is only one direction: UP! It's sometimes very steep but the views are getting better and better. Finally, you'll reach the bar "Chez Sandra" which provides a jaw dropping 360° panorama view over Paul Valley. It's the best place to have a fresh fruit juice. Without any doubt, one of the best bar views I've seen in Santo Antao.

Now the dazzling part begins and it lasts for about 15 min walk. You'll walk over the ridge until you reach the Antenna. The views are truly amazing but please be careful when walking down. It's incredibly steep and narrow!

From here, keep walking down until you reach the main Paul street. From here it's only 2 minutes to the restaurant "O Curral", famous for its organic food and juices.

After fueling up, it's about time to walk down to Cidade das Pombas. If you're looking for a well-deserved refreshment, make a stop at "Passagem" which is almost halfway between O *Curral* and *Cidade das Pombas*. You'll be able to choose among several swimming pools or the river to cool down.

11. Espongeiro – João Afonso - Coculi

Difficulty: Easy-Moderate – Duration: est. 4-5 hrs

I really enjoyed this route because of 3 reasons:

1. You get to take the spectacular Corda Road to get up to Espongeiro
2. You'll discover sceneries of Santo Antao that are very different from Paul and other hiking hotspots
3. You'll get some of the typical, jaw-dropping views of Santo Antao

I did this hike with Edson from Lima Tours and couldn't have been happier to have had him as a guide. I had so many questions about life in Santo Antao, the flowers, the traditions etc... And he answered them all! Don't hesitate to get him for your visit of the island, he speaks great English and so enjoyable to hike with.

First, you need to drive up to Espongeiro (1400m) via the spectacular Corda street. From Espongeiro, you'll make your way all the way down through the valley.

I really enjoyed the first landscapes of this hike. The rolling hills were so different from the rough valley and peaks of Paul or Cruzinha area.

You'll pass villages and single houses, but there is only one direction: down! If you get lost on the way, ask for the village of João Afonso!

From João Afonso, you'll hike along the main road to Coculi. The area has great coconuts! Make sure to get one before jumping on a *colectivo* back to Ribeira Grande town.

Please be aware that there are no restaurants on the trail until you get to Coculi, but you'll come across several *mercearias* (small shops).

I.   HOW TO SPEND 2 DAYS IN SANTO ANTAO

Porto Novo and Old Street

You can reach Santo Antao by ferry only from Mindelo (Sao Vicente). There used to be an airport in Ponta do Sol. However, it had to be closed down after a tragical accident. I recommend taking the first ferry from Mindelo in order to make the most out of your time.

The arrival in the harbor of Porto Novo might be overwhelming to you as dozens of *aluguers* (collective taxis) drivers are trying to catch your attention. That is why I recommend arranging your transfer in advance.

In Porto Novo, you can opt between the Old and the New Street to the east part of the island with towns like Ribeira Grande or Ponta do Sol. The Old Street is more expensive and winding but has the very best views! The New Street, along the coast, is cheaper but does not provide the same spectacular views.

I absolutely recommend taking the Old Road by *aluguer* (collective taxi). It is an experience on its own! The Old Road used to connect the harbor of Porto Novo to Ribeira Grande and was built in the sixties. The mountains were just too steep to build a road along the coastline.

Paved with cobblestones, it will take you to some of Santo Antao's most emblematic sites such as the Cova crater, Delgadinho and several viewpoints.

Cova Crater – Paul Valley

Cova is a volcanic caldera and on its highest point, it reaches 1.500 m. Its diameter is about 1 km and is used as fertile farmland and pastureland. There is even a small village in the caldera, which boasts particularly fertile soils due to high precipitation values carried by trade winds.

I recommend walking down from the Old Road to the crater. The path cannot be missed. It leads you to the top of the edge and from here; you will have the most breathtaking view ever on Paul Valley!

Sometimes, it might be clouded but the one-hour trail from Old Street to the crater's edge will be totally worth it! In my humble opinion, it is one of the best things to do in Cape Verde!

In case it is clouded, just enjoy the movements of the clouds. You will feel like in a cloud!

Biosfera Amor do dia

The *Biosfera Amor do dia* is one of my favorite places to stay in Santo Antao. It is completely isolated, thus perfect for travelers that are seeking peace or want to be close to several hiking trails.

The *Biosfera Amor do dia* is a hostel offering private rooms as well. My favorite part was their breakfast. They make their own bread, served with homemade butter and jams. A delight! When you do the Old Road, I recommend to stop by for a quick coffee or herbal tea.

On a sunny day, the *Biosfera Amor do dia* has the best views on the neighbor island of Sao Vicente.

From the *Biosfera Amor do dia*, you drive 10 min to the next village from which you can hike up to the top of Pico da Cruz.

With its 1.585 meters, it is the second-highest mountain of Santo Antao.

Delgadinho

Delgadinho is one of Santo Antao's most emblematic sites. You will reach the mountain ridge after 30 min from the Cova crater. Feel free to park the car on the left side (coming from Cova) and enjoy a spectacular view on the two valleys.

Also known as *Delgadim*, the straight separates the Valle Ribeira Grande and Valle Ribeira da Torre. The street is incredibly narrow and I felt dizzy when imaging how two trucks should have to pass each other!

Delgandinho is definitely essential when traveling to Santo Antao!

Ribeira Grande

Ribeira Grande is the largest municipality of Santo Antao and my favorite base to explore the rest of the island. The town, also known as *Povoação*, is the main settlement of Santo Antao since its discovery.

Even though many of Ribeira Grande's buildings are new, you can still spot several quaint examples of Portuguese architecture. One of my favorite things to do in Ribeira Grande is chasing mural art.

Sponsored by the prestigious *7Sois7Luas* festival, artists from all over Europe come to Ribeira Grande to make its streets more colorful. Just take a stroll through its backstreets and you will find several mural gems.

When in Ribeira Grandeyou cannot miss *the 7Sois7Luas* center. It is the main cultural hub on the island, providing a supporting platform for local artists.

Xoxo

Do not spend too much time in Ribeira Grande. There are still plenty of things to do and you will try to see as much as possible during your two days in Santo Antao.

I love Xoxo just for the sake of it! Pronounced "sho-sho" and only 5 km from Ribeira Grande, Xoxo forms the end of the magnificent Valle Ribeira da Torre. I invite you to take some time to marvel at the impressive setting of the village and if you are motivated, you can hike it up! I loved watching the daily grind when I was in Xoxo.

Before you reach Xoxo, you will pass along a waterfall, which might be a rewarding refreshment after all your discoveries.

In case you need to fuel up on energy, I recommend stopping at Melicia and having a *calda* (fresh sugar cane juice). It had the same effect on me as two cups of coffee! Do not have too much of it as you might end up with diarrhea! If you are very hungry, you can also have lunch here.

Lombo Branco

I bet that you will be very hungry after marveling at so much beauty! Well, I will tell you a secret spot, that only very few tourists might visit! Tell your driver or guide to take you to Lombo Branco to eat at *Casa da Sonia*. It is mandatory to book in advance (+2389795212).

The street is uneven and narrow, thus I really recommend to go with a driver (I loved *Galinha*, +2389931306) or with an *aluguer* (collective taxi).

From Lombo Branco, you will enjoy beautiful views on the sea, whilst enjoying the warm climate of Paul valley.

Besides *cachupa* (a slow cooked stew of corn, beans, cassava, sweet potato, fish or meat), the typical food you should try in Cape Verde is *igname* (yam), *garoupa* (grouper), and *grogue* (the local sugar cane alcohol). As Santo Antao is the most fertile island of the Cape Verdean archipelago, do not be surprised to stumble upon mango, passion fruit or avocado mousse for dessert! Ingredients always vary with the seasons.

Fontainhas

Fueled up with energy, you might be ready to hike again a bit! After all, Santo Antao is known as the paradise for hikers of any level!

Besides the 3-5 hrs long trail across Paul Valley from the Cova crater to Cidade das Pombas, the trail hike from Ponta do Sol to Fontainhas is one of the best hiking trails in Santo Antao.

Just drive to Ponta do Sol and leave your car there. I would never drive to Fontainhas village, unless you are going with a professional driver! The road is extremely narrow and very high up!

Fontainhas has been elected the most beautiful village of Cape Verde! I hope this provides you enough motivation to take this trek! The hike takes about 1-2 hrs from Ponta do Sol.

Go up to the cemetery of Ponta do Sol, pass along the pigsties and off you go! Just follow the trail until you reach Fontainhas. I am sure that you will fall in love with the pastel-colored houses as much as I did!

They say that Francis Drake himself has discovered Fontainhas. In addition, that he is the main reason why you can spot so many people with green or blue eyes in Fontainhas!

Please walk down to the village and enjoy the vibe of this very remote place. I highly recommend visiting *Tchu*, form *Bar Tchu*. This place will immediately make you feel at home! *Tchu* usually serves one daily menu made by ingredients of the surrounding gardens. I also recommend his self-made fruit juices.

Every other ingredient that does not grow in the fertile valley, he gets it from Ribeira Grande. Consequently, several days a week, he walks all the way to Ribeira Grande to get the beers and cokes he serves in his bar! At (too) cheap prices. With a heavy heart, I said goodbye to *Tchu* and hiked back home the same way I came from Ribeira Grande.

That is it for day 1. I recommend returning to your base and enjoying the Cape Verdean night.

Day 2 will be filled with adventures again!

DAY 2

Whether you wake up in Ribeira Grande or Ponta do Sol, a day packed with adventures, hikes and spectacular nature is awaiting you! You can choose if you prefer to do one of the top hikes in

Santo Antao or explore the island's east part with a driver like *Galinha* (+2389931306).

Valley of Lombadas

After exploring the Valley of Ribeira da Torre, it is about time to discover the Valley of Lombadas. You will drive along the streambed of the river and lush vegetation with fruta do pao (breadfruit), mangoes, avocados, etc.

The road will take you to Coculi, one of the major towns of Santo Antao. From here, I took the road to make a short detour to Cha de Pedras. Indeed, the long and thin palm trees give the village quite a picturesque entrance.

I loved to spot all the banana trees and actually, my guide explained to me that banana leaves were used to drink water and as a plate. There is no other alternative to plates than a banana leaf!

Boca De Coruja

The views are getting more spectacular with each mile! I went back from Cha de Pedras to Coculi and took the main road again to Boca do Coruja and Boca das Ambas Ribeiras. The road took me below a former bridge, Ponte do Canal, which is no longer in use.

As you continue to Lombo Santa (10 km from Ribeira Grande), you will enjoy some breathtaking views! From here, you can spot the former *caminhos vecinais* (serpentine trails) connecting the villages.

Garça

Garça is nestled on top of a steep valley that you will cross on the main road from Ribeira Grande. My main motivation to reach the village was the *merceria* (little supermarket) where you can buy traditional products such as *grogue*, mango jam or homemade cookies.

Forador

After your expedition to Vale da Ribeira Grande, it is time to have lunch. Even though you can stop at any village and have a snack, I recommend *Casa Maria* in Forador.

You will have lunch in their garden next to a water reserve, which will give you a pleasant refreshment. The views were just unbeatable and the meal I had was so delicious! *Maria* really displayed the best that Santo Antao has to offer: sweet potatoes, corn, *igname* (yam), fresh fish, fresh passion fruit juice, etc. It was a great finale for my two days in Santo Antao!

Porto Novo

If you have only two days in Santo Antao, it is unfortunately already time to head back to the harbour of Porto Novo.

From Forador, you will drive back to Ribeira Grande and take the New Road to Porto Novo harbor.

But even though you might be a bit sad that your stay in Santo Antao is already coming to an end, I recommend several stops on the New Road that will protract your departure for a bit.

Sinagoga

The first stop would be Sinagoga. The name of this village comes from a Jewish community that was expelled from Portugal and found a new home in Santo Antao. Nowadays, you can still see the impressive ruins of the synagogue.

After the Jewish community extinguished, the building was used as a sanatorium to help leprosy patients. Despite the macabre historical background, the ruins are a great photo motive. Behind the ruins, you will be spoiled with some of the best natural pools in Santo Antao!

Paul

The next stop is Paul or Cidade das Pombas that is located at the end of the natural park Paul valley. It is a quaint, lively town with several hostels and a great base to explore the hiking trails of Paul valley, one of the most fertile ones in Santo Antao.

Janela

The next stop on the New Road to Porto Novo is *Janela* (window) that got its name from the rock formation reaching into the sea. Indeed, there is a hole in the rock, forming a window to the sky and the ocean.

Before crossing the tunnel, I advise you to stop at the lighthouse (which has been fully renovated by a Spanish company). It will provide you stunning views on the rocky coastline of Santo Antao!

After Janela, the landscape becomes flatter and drier. It is such a contrast to the lush green valleys of the east part.

5.2.   BRAVA

Do you want to visit Brava, one of the remotest islands of Cape Verde? It is probably the best choice you have ever made but be ready to affront several challenges to reach the "Island of Flowers".

Indeed, the access to Brava has been very complicated for a long time: the extremely rough sea, limited and unreliable ferry connections, a closed airport, an old fishermen's boat working as a ferry, etc.

Here the good news: not only did the connections to Brava improve over the last years, but it will also be totally worth to overcome any obstacle, as you will reach a paradise for hikers and an oasis of peace!

Due to its unique mix of colorful flora, Brava is also known as the "Island of Flowers". Despite its limited size (10 km at its widest point), Brava has numerous spectacular hiking trails. You know that I am a big fan of Santo Antao for hiking, but Brava is the only island who could compete when it comes to hiking trails and spectacular views on mountains and ocean. On top, the atmosphere is even more relaxed than on Santo Antao!

The fact that it is difficult to reach and often covered in mist, created a lot of legends and adventurous stories. This feeling of being on a "lost island" is enhanced by the fact that emigration, mainly to the US, is a real problem on Brava.

Just a quick review of Brava's history. The people of Brava started working on whaleboats, and during my visit, I was lucky to meet a ship worker who had travelled all over the world! You will surely get to meet *Manuel* in one of the bars of Nova Sintra. There was and still is a massive emigration to the US and do not be surprised to find English with a strong American accent widely spoken all over the island!

How to get there:

By plane: to Fogo Airport and get the ferry to Brava. If you travel internationally, you might want to check the (often very cheap) flights to Sal or Boa Vista and take a national flight to Praia, then Fogo.

By ferry: from Fogo or Santiago. The ferry from Fogo costs around 10 €. Tickets from Fogo to Brava cannot be purchased in the harbor, but only at a travel agency like *Qualitur* on the main square of Sao Felipe. I also recommend purchasing your return ticket in advance, as selling agencies are difficult to find in Brava. From the harbour, you need to get an *aluguer* (collective taxi) to Nova Sintra.

Public Transport: *aluguers* (collective taxis) are departing from Nova Sintra at Praça Eugénio Tavares to all major towns in Brava.

Where to stay:

Hotel Pousada Nova Sintra-Brava

Djabraba's Eco-Lodge

Hotel Cruz Grande Brava ***

Residensia Ka Denxu

Where to eat:

Bar Mansa (Nova Sintra)

Hotel Djabraba's Eco-Lodge (Nova Sintra)

Residential Restaurante O CASTELO (Nova Sintra)

142

PAVLO SENA Pensao (Nova Sintra)

Pôr do Sol (Faja d'Agua)

5.2.1.EXPLORE QUAINT NOVA SINTRA

Let us start with a fun fact. Nova Sintra is the only island capital (only 1,500 inhabitants) that is not located on the sea. Bearing the name of Sintra (Portugal) due to its landscape similarities, Nova Sintra can easily be considered as one of the most beautiful town on Cape Verde (next to Sao Felipe, Fogo).

The colonial houses with their pastel-colored fronts, gardens filled with bright flowers and the main road are a delight to visit. The atmosphere is relaxing, a bit sleepy, and it rather feels like a calm village. People were so friendly and kind to me. I really think it is a pity that not so many tourists find their way to Brava.

Rua da Cultura is the main street of Nova Sintra and the best place to spot colonial architecture. The main square is Praça Eugenio Tavares, named after the famous Cape Verdean writer and founder of *morna*.

The characteristic pavilion and the creative flooring make the square one of the most charming places of Nova Sintra.

When in Nova Sintra, you should absolutely visit the *7Sois7Luas* center, which is the cultural hub of Brava. Here, you can visit exhibitions, dance on Cape Verdean music and listen to concerts.

Brava is a paradise for hikers! Despite its very limited size, you can easily spend several days on the island without doing all its trails! The wet, humid climate and mild temperatures create the ideal conditions for hiking and trekking.

It is during your hikes that you will appreciate the beauty of the *Ilha das Flores* (island of flowers). The colorful gardens will lure you with their sweet fragrances of hibiscus, Bougainville, jasmine, etc.

The two most prominent hikes in Brava are from Nova Sintra to Faja d'Agua and Fontainhas (Brava's highest village).

The trail to Fontainhas (600 m higher than Vila Nova Sintra) consists of deserted roads and starts from the road to Mira Beleza viewpoint. As the trail is not signalized, I recommend taking a guide (Rosa or Zé Duarte, 2385996115) or always asking the locals, they will be more than happy to help you out! The roundtrip takes about four hrs and you will have a fabulous view on Fogo!

Hiking down to Faja d'Agua is one of the most spectacular hikes on Brava. You can start from Nova Sintra or park your car at the Mira Beleza viewpoint. The duration from Nova Sintra is about three hours in serpentines; the cobbled path leads you along fertile, vibrant green farmland.

You will also notice that some villages have been abandoned due to emigration. You cannot get lost on that trail and Faja d'Agua is essential when traveling to Brava!

After doing the hike form Nova Sintra to Faja d'Agua, you will be craving a refreshing bath for sure! You might see that the sea is usually very brave, but I have good news for you! Faja d'Agua has some of the most gorgeous natural pools that I have ever seen on the entire Cape Verdean archipelago!

Cross the village of Faja d'Agua and follow the signage. They'relocated one km from the village. The scenery is breathtaking! In my humble opinion, it is one of the best things to do in Cape Verde!

In addition, Faja d'Agua itself is worth a stop. With origins going back to 1747, the village was famous for being a landing port for whale ships coming from the United States. Brava is by far the island with the strongest American influence. The *Monumento aos Emigrantes* erected in 1993 is a symbol for the massive emigration towards the United States.

145

The location is absolutely privileged. Sheltered by the mountains, you will enjoy a peaceful view on the sea, framed by palm trees.

I also recommend to have lunch in Faja d'Agua, for example in *Casa Julinha* (+238 9850079), to absorb the relaxing vibe. Just give *Rosa Borges* a call (+2389827680) and she will take care of the rest!

5.2.4. VISIT THE SPOOKY, ABANDONED AIRPORT OF ESPERADINHA

The abandoned airport of Esperadinha is located one km after the natural swimming pools of Faja D'Agua. It opened in 1992 as the only airport of Brava, but it had to close in 2004 because of the strong winds and the short landing strip.

The shutdown also marked the beginning of the decline of Faja D'Agua.

However, the former Brava Airport is a great place to visit and do a mandatory "flying photo" on the former landing strip. Again, you will have impressive views on the rocky coastline of Brava!

5.2.5. ENJOY THE LOCAL CAPE VERDEAN MUSIC

The music of Cape Verde is its real richness! The variety and quantity of singers, composers and musicians on each island is a thing that I can never get used to!

Even though some of the most popular musical forms are *Funaná, Coladeira, Batuque* and *Cabo love, morna* is still the most prominent one. Lyrics are in Cape Verdean creole and include

146

instruments like *cavaquinho* (a small Portuguese string instrument in the European guitar family, clarinet, accordion, violin, piano and guitar. Some songs are deeply melancholic, whereas others are joyful.

I highly recommend assisting to a musical performance of the *7Sois7Luas* band. They compose their own songs and the lead singer, *Rosa Borges*, is a real phenomenon! In the shortest time, she manages to captivate the audience with her vibrant voice and glowing aura!

Concerts take place in the cultural hub *7Sois7Luas* center in Nova Sintra where you can also have dinner with the musicians after the show.

You will get a deep insight in the Cape Verdean culture and particularly its music during a truly unique and eye-opening experience. The cost for a performance is about 100 €. Just give *Rosa Borges* (+2389827680) or *Zé Duarte* (+2385996115) a call and they will take care of this for you.

5.2.6. VISIT A CHEESE FACTORY IN CACHAÇO

One of the top things to do in Brava is to visit a local cheese factory. The village of Cachaço is famous for its cheese production and there used to be more than two cheese factories. However, due to the dryness, they were closed during my visit.

Still, you can go to Cachaço (the ride from Nova Sintra is so picturesque!) and ask for *Jacqueline*. She can give you a little demonstration of how typical goat cheese is produced since several generations.

No additives are used to produce the cheese that is produced with milk from the same day and that they sell for one € each. For fermentation, they use a liquid gained from the stomach of a baby goat. In a few hours, the milk is coagulating and ready to become cheese.

Assisting the cheese making process gave me a valuable insight in the daily grind of Brava's inhabitants.

5.2.7.GO VIEWPOINT HOPPING

The *miradouros* (viewpoints) of Brava are a class of their own. There are several ones spread all over the island and each time, you will think that is the most beautiful one!

Some of them will provide you a dramatic view on the staggering deep valleys, while others, towards Fogo, will leave you in awe with nature's magnitude! Indeed, the view from Brava on Fogo is unbeatable!

- Matogrande Village: You will have the best view on Fogo from Matogrande village. It will catch your breath for sure! The village is also the starting point to hike to Garça.
- Matogrande Viewpoint: On the road from Nova Sintra to Matrogrande, I recommend to stop at the *miradouro* (viewpoint) of Matogrande, from which you will enjoy a spectacular view on Nova Sintra. There is also a *grogue* (grog) factory close to the viewpoint, but I ignore whether it is open for visitors.
- Mirabeleza Viewpoint: Probably the most spectacular viewpoint is the *miradouro Mirabeleza* ("look at beauty") on the way to Cachaço. The views on the lush green valley and the sea are breathtaking! It is also the starting point for your trek to Faja d'Agua.

5.2.8.ENJOY PEOPLE WATCHING IN FURNAS

This might sound awkward as an activity, but actually, it was one of my favorite things to do on Brava. Just sit down and watch the daily grind go by.

I was marveling at the vibrant mix of people in Brava. It is fascinating how many kids have blue or green eyes with a dark skin! My guide explained that it was due to the Portuguese and Italian legacy. As the island of Brava is so remote and difficult to reach, this extraordinary mix has been preserved over centuries.

My favorite place to observe the daily grind was in Cachaço, Nova Sintra and Furna.

Furna, the main harbor of Brava has a different vibe than the other municipalities on the island. It is a bit busier, due to the arrivals and departures of the ferry. Furna is a typical fishermen village and the colorful house fronts add a lot of charm.

5.3.   FOGO

The landscape of Fogo is one of the most dramatic ones of the Cape Verdean archipelago. The entire island is dominated by the imposing volcano Pico do Fogo. The highly active volcano has a strong impact on the agriculture, lifestyle and daily grind. Indeed, life under the threat of a volcanic eruption can be extreme!

With its 2,829 meters, Fogo does not only have the highest peak of the Cape Verdean archipelago, but it is also one of the highest islands in the world! The Pico do Fogo, the volcano's peak, is also one of the most active volcanoes on this planet! Its last eruption dates only back to 2014! Living under the threat of a volcanic eruption obviously shapes daily life and even the local's sense of humor (according to my guide).

During the last eruption in 2014, the village of Chã das Caldeiras, built inside the volcanic crater on black sand, has been destroyed! However, the people from Chã had (and still have!) a very deep connection with the volcano. Therefore, they decided to go back to the crater and rebuilt the village from scratch! Some even built their new houses on top of their former, now destroyed ones!

The "lost" village of Chã das Caldeiras is thus an absolute must on your trip to Fogo!

Even though Fogo has a diameter of only 25 km, it is extreme when it comes to height!

How to get there:

By plane: To Fogo Airport from Praia International Airport. If you travel internationally, you might want to check the (often very cheap) flights to Sal or Boa Vista and take a national flight to Praia.

By boat: From Brava or Santiago island. The ferry to Fogo from/to Brava costs around 10 €.

How to get around:

Airport Transfers: A taxi from the ferry port to Sao Filipe is around 400 Esc (+/- 3,63 €) and from the airport, 300 Esc (+/- 2,72 €). Prices may vary!

Rent a car: To rent a car, feel free to contact one of the local agencies: *Qualitur*, *Zebra Travel* or ONG *Cospe*.

Public Transport: *Aluguers* (collective taxis) are departing from Sao Felipe (Francisco Assis square) to all major towns on the island.

Where to stay:

    Casas Do Sol ***

    Casa Colonial Koenig ***

    Tortuga B&B

    The Colonial Guest House

    Hotel Xaguate ****

In the volcano crater (!)

    casa alcindo

    Pensao Casa José Doce

    Casa Marisa 2.0

5.3.1. HIKE THE FOGO VOLCANO

The Pico do Fogo volcano dominates the entire island and obviously, it is essential when visiting Fogo! Whereas the coast is very fertile and with lush green vegetation, the immediate surroundings of the volcano are deep, black and either composed of lava or sand.

The moonscape and colossal shape of the Pico do Fogo will affect you from the first moment you spot it! The contorted lava flows will let you feel very, very tiny. Indeed, I never felt as small as in Fogo! The imposing power of the peak, the crater and lava flows were overwhelming!

The Fogo Natural Park is about a 45 min. drive from the colorful capital of São Felipe. If you want to hike up the volcano, I recommend contacting *Alcindo Silva*, my guide for the hike (*Alcindo6@gmail.com, +2389921409*). He lives in the volcanic village of Cha das Caldeiras and knows the volcano like his pocket! His knowledge about Fogo's endemic plants and his kindness does the rest.

Hikes to the volcano usually start very early (+/- 5 am!) as there is no shape during the entire trail. The hikes can also be done my beginner/medium hikers. It takes about 3-4 hrs to get up to the top and only 30 min to get down. It is great fun to run down in the volcanic sand!

The village of Chã das Caldeiras (Plain of the Caldeiras) is truly unique in the world! With a community of only 700 inhabitants, the village is located in the black crater of the volcano Pico do Fogo. It is the highest village of Cape Verde and it is the only area in Cape Verde, which produces a large quantity of qualitative wine.

The village has been destroyed during the last volcanic eruption in 2014. However, the locals have a very strong connection to this unique place. They came back and re-built the village from scratch! *Alcindo* told me that some people re-built their homes on the lava covering their former homes!

In that sense, Chã das Caldeiras is a very special experience, even only to roam around and spot the typical round houses.

However, you cannot leave this unusual place without visiting the cooperative and doing a wine tasting.

Indeed, Chã das Caldeiras is one of the very few places producing qualitative wine, a tradition that is more than 100 years old! It is only exported to the other Cape Verdean islands, not internationally.

The wines of Chã are full-bodied and rich in color. The *Associaçao* (cooperative) produces white, red and rosé wines. You should definitely try the *vinho passito*, a sweet, Moscatel like wine. The wine from Chã is a 100 % organic product as no insecticides or pesticides are used. Only rainwater is used for irrigation.

It might be surprising that grapes (as welle as apples, cactus fruit, etc.) grow in this bare, black landscape. However, the cool and humid nights, as well as the hot and dry days are perfect for viticulture. The volcanic soils are particularly rich.

The *Associaçao* has rooms for guests, offers guided tours of their wine cellar, and organizes wine tastings. It is definitely a must and a highlight when visiting Fogo! The wine cellars are located on your left when coming from Sao Felipe and after passing the Pico do Fogo.

A wine wasting can be organized in the *Wine Cooperative*. If you want to enjoy the homemade wine of the inhabitants of Cha das Caldeiras, look out for the *Manekom* sign when leaving Portela. *Manekom* is the name of their homemade wine.

Even if it might sound contradictory, the dark black land of Fogo has one of the richest soils on the Cape Verdean archipelago! Indeed the volcanic soil is particularly fertile and it is the main reason why people take the high risk to live so close to the crater.

This richness manifests itself mainly via a large variety of food.

Each of the three municipalities is famous for a particular product. Sao Felipe and the surrounding villages are famous for goat cheese, Santa Catarina is well known for wine and goat cheese and Mosteiros is the fruit garden of the island. Here, you can find all kinds of fruits like mangoes and the town produces most of the island's coffee exports.

Besides *cachupa* (a slow cooked stew of corn, beans, cassava, sweet potato, fish or meat), two of the most typical dishes of the island are *djagacida* (made of corn, fish and beans) and *pastel de milho* (corn cake). When it comes to drinks, you cannot miss trying *bissap* (a fruit juice made of hibiscus flower) and *calabaceira*, a juice gained from the baobab fruit.

Upon demand, a typical lunch can be organized in the volcano crater! Just call *Rosa Avelino* (+2389871589) for a "*para almoço na cratera do vulcão*" ("lunch in the volcano crater").

The capital of Fogo, São Felipe, will lure you with its colonial charm. It is the largest municipality of the island and it is easy to fall in love with its relaxing vibe. It is also the perfect base to explore the island. On top, São Felipe is only 20 min away from the airport and 10 min from the harbour, which connects Fogo to Praia and Brava.

São Felipe is considered the second oldest town of the Cape Verdean archipelago. During the 19th century, São Felipe was particularly wealthy due to its cotton, wine and coffee exports. Still nowadays, 70 % of the existing houses in São Felipe date back from this golden age.

My favorite part of São Felipe are the soft, pastel-colored housefronts and the quaint plazas. Since 2000, many of the houses have been carefully renovated. I was lucky to meet the mayor of São Felipe and blown away by his energy and the innovative projects that he is developing for São Felipe!

Due to its vast renovations, the colonial city center of São Felipe (also known as "Bila Baixa") reminds me of the colonial towns of La Laguna (Tenerife) and Granada (Nicaragua). Some of the house fronts have been decorated with colorful streetart.

The wooden balconies, richly decorated house fronts and colorful squares are creating a particularly picturesque scene. The most emblematic square is the Praca 12 de septembro with its wooden pavilion and the majestic city hall. Two other places you cannot miss are the light-blue church of *Nossa Senhora da Conceicao* and the busy market hall.

The square of Francisco de Assis is key as it hosts the post office and the most important bus stop in town.

5.3.5.LISTEN TO LOCAL MUSIC

São Felipe is also home to the *7Sois7Luas* center, a cultural hub supporting local musicians and painters. The center does not only serve typical Cape Verdean food, but also organizes many events throughout the year. It is a vital place to promote and support local artists!

Indeed, the local cultural scene is threatened by emigration to other islands or even the US. As salaries might be more attractive abroad, many artists from Fogo choose money over the local art scene.

The *7Sois7Luas* center wants to counterbalance this trend and offers a perspective to local artists and musicians.

An absolute highlight is to organize a social event with Cape Verdean music! You will not only get an authentic insight into the Cape Verdean hospitality, but you will also support the local community. It is thus a perfect example of sustainable travel!

5.3.6. BUY GOAT CHEESE

Fogo is synonym to goat cheese when it comes to food. Even though goat cheese is produced on many Cape Verdean islands, the cheese of Fogo is particularly famous!

Goat cheese is a production process with a long tradition. No additives besides milk and the fermentation trigger (a liquid gained of the baby goat's stomach) are used. The cheese that you buy is often only 24-48 hrs old!

You can easily buy goat cheese on the little farms along the road. Just stop at the "queijo" signs.

Thanks to the circular road, you can easily do an around-the-island tour. It will be a spectacular trip, as you will appreciate the diversity of the island ranging from vibrant green plantations to dark lava soil and a lovely countryside with farmhouses.

You can either ask one of the local tour agencies to organize a trip or ask your host if she/he knows somebody who could take you around. The local agencies are *Qualitur*, *Zebra Travel* and *ONG Cospe*. Some of their offers include packages to Santo Anto and Brava.

Some of the unmissable stops during your island roundtrip are Mosteiros and Sao Lourenco, which offers a great view on Brava.

5.3.8. HIKE FROM CHA DAS CALDEIRAS TO MOSTREIROS

If you think that hiking up the Mount Fogo volcano would be the only thing to do on Fogo, you could not be more wrong!

There is another spectacular trail waiting for you from Cha das Caldeiras to Mostreiros.

I particularly liked the extremely saturated green colors of Mother Nature. They seem even brighter after experiencing the baren, black sands of the Mount Fogo crater.

The hike takes five hrs and is intermediate level. Ask your host in Cha das Caldeiras to bring your luggage to Mostreiros.

A taxi from Mostreiros to Sao Filipe costs 6.000 Esc (+/- 54,46 €)

5.3.9.ENJOY SOME BEACH TIME

Even though Fogo is not particularly famous for its beaches, you do not have to abstain from a refreshing bath! If you are based in Sao Felipe, you will be tempted to go to the small beach of Praia da Bila, consisfomer ting of black sand, and located below the emblematic Praça Serpa Pinto square.

However, the locals prefer the beach at the harbour Porto de Vale de Cavaleiros, about 4 km in the north of Sao Filipe, which is the island's westernmost point. In spite of the harbour, the water's cleaner and the sea is not so rough. The most popular beach of the island is Ponta da Salina in São Jorge.

It can be reached by the Sao Jorge *aluguer* (collective taxi). Ask the driver to be dropped off there and check what time the *aluguer* (collective taxi) is returning.

Located between Santa Luzia and Sal, São Nicolau is a quaint, sophisticated place that impresses with its pristine sceneries and uncontaminated nature.

From all the islands of the archipelago, São Nicolau is perhaps your best bet if you want to avoid mass tourism and enjoy sustainable holidays in Cape Verde.

This tranquil island has somehow managed to stay off the tourist paths. Therefore, it is an excellent place for soaking up the sun, swimming, and snorkeling.

If you look for a local guide, I recommend Ivanildo Fortes (+238 978 9796 or +238 950 2131), he organizes boat trips and turtle watching tours as well.

How to get there:

By boat: From Sao Vicente or Santiago with CV *Interilhas*

By plane: From Santiago or Sal to Sao Nicolau Airport

Where to stay:

Budget:

> Bed & breakfast Regina

> Los Cuartos Man Pretinha

Mid-Range:

> Edificio Magico

Family-Friendly:

> Zena Star

Luxury:

> Casa Patio

---

1. HIKE THE MONTE GORDO

The Parque Natural Monte Gordo is a real treat for hiking enthusiasts! This magnificent mountain has a volcanic origin and rises to over 4,300 feet above the sea level!

Not only you can enjoy spectacular views from the top, but also on your way up to the summit, you will be able to discover a variety of endemic species of both flora and fauna.

How to get there: Monte Gordo is located less than 7 km west of the island's capital, Ribeira Brava, and is easily accessible by car, foot, scooter and bike.

2. MARVEL AT CARBEIRINHO

Have you ever wondered where the science-fiction filmmakers find those breathtaking, unearthly landscapes to film their movies? Well, Carbeirinho is one of them!

The harsh waters and winds have shaped the stunning lunar scenery. The color of the rocks makes it easy to admire the various layers of sediments.

Undeniably, if you do not see Carbeirinho during your stay, you cannot say that you have actually seen Sao Nicolau!

How to get there: There is no public transport to Carbeirinho but you can easily reach this location with a taxi from Tarrafal.

3. SWIM AT BAIXO ROCHA

Tarrafal might be a small village, but it boasts an impressive number of natural wonders! Once you have visited Carbeirinho, you can continue this idyllic day swimming at Baixo Rocha.

Way off the beaten track, this remote beach can only be accessed from a dusty road or from the sea. However, you will have one of the best beach experiences in Cape Verde!

It is definitely well worth the effort of getting there! Completely free of human civilization, this small patch of bliss impresses with turquoise waters and expanses of white sand.

A true little heaven for sunbathers, swimmers and snorkelers!

How to get there: From Tarrafal, take the dusty road towards Casa Aquaria. The remote beach is around one hour's walk from the village, and it can only be reached on foot.

4. VISIT RIBEIRA BRAVA

Stretching along the crystalline shore, Ribeira Brava is São Nicolau's capital, but do not expect any big-city rhythms in this place!

This quaint little town awaits with picturesque cobblestone streets and colorful colonial houses. The perfect place to witness the vibrant West African lifestyle in all its glory!

The paved streets are filled with merchants selling crafted goods, fruits, vegetables and street foods.

The Praça do Torreiro church square with the *Igreja Nossa Senhora do Rosário* is not only an important landmark. Here, you can also find many restaurants and bars for a well-deserved break.

Nature surrounds the city, and the lovely park, which is nestled in the town center, is an excellent place to explore in the afternoon.

How to get there: By plane from Praia, Santiago and Sal.

5. EXPLORE RIBEIRA PRATA

Ribeira Prata is a small settlement in the northwest side of the island, situated around 10 km north from Tarrafal.

Counting less than 400 souls, this quaint village is one of the most authentic places in Cape Verde, and the gateway to some of the best hiking trails on the island. No doubt, a must for both history lovers and hiking enthusiasts!

It is a great place for hiking but please make sure to be covered with a Cape Verde travel insurance! I got mine at HeyMondo and I love it for its easy setup.

How to get there: By foot, car or taxi from Tarrafal.

6. VISIT THE VILLAGE OF PREGUIÇA

Preguiça is another stunning settlement to visit while exploring Sao Nicolau.

Situated at a stone's throw away from Ribeira Brava, this fishing village overlooks the turquoise waters of the ocean from the rugged cliffs on which it is perched.

Unlike the archipelago's major towns, Preguiça does not boast colonial-style architecture, but exploring this place is essential if you want to enjoy some of the best views over the Atlantic Ocean.

How to get there: Situated close to Ribeira Brava, Preguiça is home to the island's only airport, and it can be easily reached by car or taxi from the island's capital.

7. VISIT THE VILLAGE OF TARRAFAL

Nestled in the western part of the island, Tarrafal is the island's main tourist hub and the main port of the Sao Nicolau.

Obviously, the best things to do here are beach-related; from sunbathing to swimming or diving.

Exploring the town is worthy too. Livelier than Ribeira Brava, Tarrafal boasts a bustling nightlife, loads of bars and restaurants, as well as some of the best hotels on the island. In addition, if you learn a few creole phrases, you will even have the chance to connect with the local people!

Casa Aquario and the Black Fish Club Museu Da Pesca are two of the most popular places where to grab a drink or a bite, while Edificio Magico, located a few steps away from the main beach, and could be a great choice if you are looking for a good hotel in Sao Nicolau.

How to get there: By ferry from all islands or by car/taxi from Ribeira Brava.

8. PHOTOGRAPH ANCIENT DRAGON TREES

Did you know that Sao Nicolau is famous all around the world? This off-the-beaten-track island fascinates biologists and nature lovers alike with its unique dragon trees.

This endemic tree species grows majorly in the Fajã valley, a place of breathtaking beauty where not only you can admire these amazing trees, but where you can also snap the perfect "Insta-worthy" shot!

How to get there: By hiking or bike from Ribeira Brava.

9. SWIM IN THE NATURAL SWIMMING POOLS

Swimming in Sao Nicolau goes way beyond plunging into the ocean! On the northern side of the island, Juncalinho awaits you with its natural basalt swimming pools.

Impressing with their transparent, blue-green waters, and overlooking the ocean, they almost feel like a five-star resort experience! No doubt; an experience to enjoy on those days when the ocean is calm!

How to get there: By minibus from Ribeira Brava.

10. VISIT THE FERTILE FAJÃ VALLEY

Besides admiring dragon trees and snapping amazing photos, exploring the Fajã valley is also essential while visiting Sao Nicolau. This fertile land is home to many endemic species, as well as a paradise for birds.

The main hiking trail leads to Ribeira Brava. You could also hire a local guide to explore some off the beaten track itineraries. No matter your choice, rest assured that you would have the experience of your lifetime!

How to get there: By foot or bike, from Ribeira Brava.

6. IN-DEPTH: THE CULTURE ISLANDS

6.1.   SAO VICENTE

Sao Vicente is much more than Mindelo! Although 93 % of the island's population lives in its capital, Sao Vicente has a lot to offer to its visitors.

In addition, if you need to disconnect from the city's tumult and its almost infinite leisure options, an excursion to the countryside of São Vicente is exactly what you need! After living on the island for about two months, I cannot wait to share my tips with you!

To me, Sao Vicente is one of the most diverse islands of Cape Verde as it has things to do for any type of traveler! Whether you are looking for relaxing beach bars, indulging in food, shopping, watersports or culture, you can do it all in Sao Vicente!

How to get there:

By plane to Sao Vicente International Airport.

How to get around: in Sao Vicente?

Mindelo can be explored by foot.

If you want to visit the island, I recommend traveling by *aluguers* (collective taxis) that depart from Praça d'Estrela.

If you are short in time, I recommend booking an island tour with Viator.

Where to stay:

Budget

Solar Windelo ***
Arla Residential

Mid-Range

Pousada B&B Le Gourmet

Family-Friendly

Morabeza Deluxe Sea View

Something Special

Aquiles Eco Hotel
Pont'Agua Hotel ****

Luxury

Flag Hotel Foya Branca ****
Terra Lodge
Oasis Porto Grande ****

6.1.1. VISIT MINDELO, CULTURAL CAPITAL OF CABO VERDE

Also known as the cultural capital of the archipelago, Mindelo is easy to fall in love with. It has a very particular atmosphere that you cannot find anywhere else in Cape Verde. It's festive, loud and colorful!

Where to Stay in Mindelo, São Vicente

Budget

Laginha Beach Guest House
Residencial Monte Cara
Simabo's Backpacker's Hostel *(Support their animal association by staying here)*

Mid-Range

Hotel Alto Fortim ***
The Don Paco Hotel ***

Family-Friendly

Apart Hotel Avenida ***

Eco-Friendly

Terra Lodge

Luxury

Pousada Monte Cara
Casa Branca ****
Pont d'Agua Hotel ***
Oasis Porto Grande ****
Terra Lodge

IS MINDELO, CAPE VERDE SAFE?

By all the affinity I felt for Mindelo and its liveliness, it gets a little minusdue to safety issues. Often, the Capeverdean boys would try to get my attention as a girl.

When walking alone, I got harshly stopped in the streets. Boys shouting after me of staring at me as if I'd be a pink elephant were part of daily life.

At some point, it just gets annoying! In several situations, I felt unsafe, i.e. when youngsters were running at me to ask for some escudos and were too insisting. By the time I just learned to ignore them and move on. The best strategy is just not to pay them any attention and continue your path.

1. FOLLOW THE FOOTSTEPS OF CESARIA EVORA

Due to its most important citizen, Cesária Évora, Mindelo reached worldwide fame for being the cradle of *Morna*, the traditional

Capeverdean music genre. Many singers from *São Vicente* popularized *Morna* all over the world.

But none of them reached the status of the legendary "Barefoot Diva", the queen of *Morna*. Many singers following her footsteps are from Mindelo and made it a hub for Capeverdean culture.

Next to the major pink building at *Avenida Lisboa*, you'll find the Cesaria Evora Museum. It's located within her house and you'll most likely meet some of her relatives. I was lucky enough to meet her daughter and I consider this encounter remarkable still today.

2. ENJOY MINDELO'S MUSIC SCENE

The city is full of music bars, art galleries, and creative ateliers (CapVertDesign+Artesanato, Arte d'Cretcheu, Tchalé Figueira Gallery). Lampposts are packed with posters announcing cultural activities.

Almost every weekend, you can attend a concert by a major Capeverdean singer coming back to his home place to sing for his people.

I truly enjoyed the mixture of a lively art scene and simple street life. At every corner, market women are selling fish, caring containers with fresh herbs and sweets on their heads. Others sell their hand-made African dresses

3. GO SHOPPING AT THE MARKETS IN MINDELO

Despite being a quite smelly affair, alone the fish market is worth a visit. You'll hardly get this full immersion to authentic Capeverdean life anywhere else. The same happens in the city market.

In all there are 3 markets in Mindelo:

- Old Market Building

- the Fish Market

- the open market on Praça Estrela

Set in a photogenic building, the market ladies will try to sell you, in a sometimes a bit forceful way, their homemade banana and papaya jams.

Or some coco *ponche*, one of the most traditional foods to enjoy when in Cape Verde. Prices are not as low as you might expect since everything needs to be imported from neighbor island Santo Antao.

4. GO LOUD AT MINDELO'S CARNIVAL

The city center of Mindelo can easily be discovered in a few hours. The colorful house fronts and their colonial-style will let you feel a step closer to tropical Brazil.

Sao Vicente has something else in common with Brazil: The Carnival of Mindelo is supposed to be the best of the Capeverdean archipelago. It is one of the top things to do when visiting Mindelo.

Carnival in Mindelo starts right after New Years' when the Mandinga groups take over the streets on Sunday. The official groups prepare their parade and music and drums can be heard in the streets of Mindelo almost every night.

The Tuesday of Carnival four groups battle for the title in the amazing parade competition with thousands of spectators along the route.

It's an amazing party that you shouldn't miss when you happen to be in Mindelo during January or February.

5. GO PARTY AT MINDELO NIGHTLIFE

They say that Mindelo's nightlife can compete directly with Praia's. But many locals told me that it has changed a lot in the last years: poverty increased and there's hardly any night bar where locals and tourists mingle.

I tried to access some local clubs, but I went through a few awkward situations to get there. Many are located in dark side streets. Since then, I desisted of the idea of clubbing in Mindelo.

175

But if you're up to a quieter night out, then Mindelo has plenty of options. I enjoyed the creative atmosphere at the Library "Nho Djunga". The guitarist of Cesária Évora frequently gives concerts here and it's the only place where I saw Capeverdean people mix with tourists to listen to some authentic *Morna*.

Another option is *Casa da Morna*. It belongs to famous singer Tito Paris who often stops by to give a gig. To start the night, I recommend Passion Fruit or Kiwi Caipirinhas at Elvis' Bar. They are simply the best!

6. ENJOY CAPE VERDEAN FOOD IN MINDELO, SAO VICENTE

When traveling to Cape Verde, enjoying the local food is a must! The traditional Cape Verdean food is a great mix of influences from Europe (particularly Portugal), the African continent and Brazil.

However, more and more you can spot international cuisine in Mindelo too.

The most popular food from Cape Verde is without any doubt Cachupa.

To eat the traditional **Cachupa**, Cape Verde's most famous dish, I recommend Dokas. Set right next to the ships of the marina, its Cachupa is always fresh at an unbeatable price of 1,50 €.

- Elvis Restobar – Mindelo

- Chave d'Ouro – Mindelo

- Pastelaria Morabeza – Mindelo

- Dokas – Mindelo

- Restaurante Hamburg – Calhau

- Chez Loutcha – Mindelo, Calhau

- Onda Morna Restaurante – Mindelo

7. GO SOUVENIR SHOPPING IN LOCAL SHOPS

You are looking for some unique souvenirs for your beloved ones at home?

The good news is that Mindelo hardly boats any shops selling souvenirs "made in China" that you could basically buy anywhere.

There are plenty of artisan shops where you can purchase locally made, artisan goods. This is one of the best ways to practice sustainable tourism in Cape Verde since you are directly supporting the local community.

I leave you with a list of the best small, independent shops in Mindelo, Cape Verde:

- Lucy's (next to the main supermarket in Mindelo)

- Trapos Polibel – Mindelo

- Swell D'Sul – Mindelo

- CapVertDesign+Artesanato

- Atelier Violão Aniceto Gomes – Monte Sossego, district Tras de Cemiterio (for handmade Cape Verdean guitars)

- Tchalé Figueira Art Gallery

8. DO A GUIDED TOUR WITH A LOCAL

Do you want to get a unique glimpse into Cape Verdean culture? Often, it's hard to get a look behind the scenes when you don't speak the language.

That's why it's a great idea to do a guided tour with a local guide who will show you the best-hidden gems of the city. On top, you'll learn a lot about the local culture, history and in most cases, you make a great connection with the guide.

9. VISIT THE BEST BUILDINGS IN TOWN

Mindelo boasts an incredible history and during many decades Mindelo has been one of the most important harbors in the world. Even though its role slowly declined, you can still witness plenty of the town's former wealth.

Many of the prettiest buildings in Mindelo have been inspired by Portuguese architecture and can be qualified as colonial style. However, what I like best about them are their colorful, often pastel-colored housefronts.

They make such great photo motives!

Here some of the buildings that are a must on any Mindelo itinerary.

- Torre de Belem

- Centro Cultural do Mindelo

- Palacio do Povo

- Town Hall

10. RELAX AT PRAIA LAGINHA

If Mindelo seems the dooryard of Brazil, then Laginha beach must be the Capeverdean version of Copacabana. With its white sandy beach and turquoise water, it's not only a popular photo motive but also one of the prettiest city beaches I've seen so far.

Indeed, hitting the most famous beach of Mindelo, Praia Laginha is a must on any Mindelo visit.

It's here where the locals meet in order to exchange the latest gossips, where the girls show their newest bikinis and men trying to impress the ladies.

If you are not in the mood for a swim, then there are plenty of beach bars to choose from. I recommend having a caipirinha with *grogue* and for a second you'll think that you're in Brazil.

6.1.2. SUNDAYS IN CALHAU, SAO VICENTE

Calhau is a little fishing village on the east coast of Sao Vicente. It takes you 30 min to get there from Mindelo by *aluguer* (collective taxi, departing from Praca d'Estrela, 1,50 €). During the week, Calhau is almost desert. Not many tourists get lost here, except maybe some surfers waiting for the perfect wave on Praia Grande.

However, on Sundays, Calhau attracts many visitors due to its excellent fish restaurants. The most famous ones are *Restaurante Hamburg* and *Chez Loutcha Residencial Restaurant & Bar*. *Restaurante Hamburg* is known all over the island for its delicious seafood and fish barbecue. The baby octopus is amazing and portions are huge! You will leave *Restaurante Hamburg* as a very happy person!

Chez Loutcha Residencial Restaurant & Bar offers a traditional buffet and live Cape Verdean music on Sundays.

A free transport departs at 12h30 at *Chez Loutcha Residencial Restaurant & Bar* on Praca d'Estrela in Mindelo and brings you back after lunch. For 18 €, you will have a Sunday brunch of a lifetime!

In order to burn all these calories, I would walk to Praia Grande (20 min.). It has golden sand and the views on the bay and the mountains are stunning! Please, be careful if you go for a swim, as the tides are very strong here!

6.1.3. HIKE THE MONTE VERDE

It is by far the best hiking trail of São Vicente! Monte Verde (Green Mountain) is the island's highest mountain and lives up to its name! It is one of the few places of São Vicente covered with lush green vegetation. You get there by *aluguer* (collective taxi) from Mindelo, Praca d'Estrela.

The driver will drop you off on the road to Salamanca/Bahía das Gatas. Monte Verde is towering just in front of you. A paved road will take you up to its peak covered by antennas and parabolas. It is an easy hike and it will take you about two hrs to get there.

From the top, you will have a great panorama view on Sao Vicente, Santo Antao, and Santa Luzia, and on very clear days, you can even see Sao Nicolau! For me, there is no better way to disconnect from Mindelo's tumult!

For those who still want to hike around, I can recommend Monte Cara (Face Hill). It got its name due to its lines resembling apparently the profile of George Washington.

6.1.4. SWIM AND DANCE IN BAHIA DAS GATAS

Baía das Gatas is known all over the Cape Verdean archipelago for its music festival. The most important names of the national music scene give concerts on a big stage next to the beach.

The big event takes place in August and is transmitted directly on national TV. Nowadays, it is one of the most important events of the Cape Verdean music business and a coveted platform for newcomers.

Throughout the rest of the year, Baía das Gatas is partly deserted. The place is packed with holiday homes, which are only inhabited during the weekends.

However, Baía das Gatas holds a hidden gem, which is a green lagoon. It is very likely that you will be all alone to enjoy the beauty of this place!

6.1.5. PRACTICE WATERSPORTS IN SAO PEDRO

Sao Pedro is a great getaway from Mindelo (15 min. by *aluguer*, 1 €). Its beach is simply enormous and almost empty! Sao Pedro preserved its fishing atmosphere, despite being literally at a stone's throw from the airport.

In the village's center, you will see how the colorful boats are being repaired.

On the beach, fishermen help each other to bring their boats to the shore. Their boats are full of the freshest fish: *buzio*, *garoupa* (groupers), *esmedregal* (cobia), and sometimes, even tuna fish!

Sao Pedro is famous for its perfect conditions for windsurfing. Boards can be rented at the station, but you better had some experience since the tides are very strong! I preferred to enjoy the peace and the views of *Hotel Foya Branca*.

For hikers, I recommend to trek to the lighthouse of Sao Pedro. The views are just breathtaking!

As of October 2020, a beach bar has opened just in front of the main village. It's managed by a young French couple and they serve amazing *pastel* here.

6.1.5. GO TO THE MOVIES AND HAVE SOME CAIPIRINHAS

Mindelo has almost an infinite number of leisure options! Each night, you can assist concerts in its numerous bars. My favorite is *Livraria Nho Djunga* where one of *Cesaria Evora*'s guitarists gives frequent concerts.

Casa da Morna, belonging to famous singer *Tito Paris*, has specialized on the traditional music style called "*Morna*".

Thursdays in Mindelo are my favorite ones! Each Thursday night, the *Centro Cultural do Mindelo* has its cinema night. The entrance is free and the movie is announced a few days in advance.

All of them are in OV with Portuguese subtitles. A great way to improve your Portuguese!

After the movie, you should go over to *Elvis — Restobar*. His kiwi and maracujá caipirinhas are famous all over town!

The capital of Sao Vicente holds a few hidden spots to make great qualitative souvenir shopping. One of them is definitely *CapVertDesign + Artesanato*. The shop is worth a visit, even if you are not looking for gifts. It gives a fantastic overview of traditional Cape Verdean crafts.

Many young design talents use this shop as a platform to reach a foreign public. If you are looking for CDs of Cape Verde's most important stars, you are in the right place!

Just in front of the fish market (please do visit, even if the smell might hold you back for 1 sec.!), a local jewelry designer sells beautiful individual pieces made out of natural material like banana leaves, mussels, or pea-pods.

Another great place to find local art and craft is *Art d'Cretcheu* inside the *Centro Cultural do Mindelo*.

I also loved to visit the fruit and vegetable market on Praca d'Estrela. On the end of the square, inside the tiny concrete barracks, you can order tailor-made clothes at the African tailors. I could not resist and got myself a tailor-made dress and lovely skirt. All at unbeatable prices!

6.1.7. ENJOY THE LOCAL FOOD

During your trip to Sao Vicente, you cannot miss indulging in local food!

Some of the best restaurants are:

- *Elvis Bar & Restaurante* (Mindelo)
- *Chave d'Ouro* (Mindelo)
- *Casa Café* (Mindelo)
- *Restaurante Hamburg* (Calhau)
- *Chez Loutcha* (Mindelo and Calhau)
- *Dokas* (Mindelo)
- *Onda Morna Restaurante* (Mindelo)

6.1.8. ENJOY THE BEACHES

Sao Vicente is home to marvelous beaches. There seems to be a beach for any type of traveller. Whether you prefer to chill out at a cocktail bar or get active with watersports, there is a beach for your needs!

The most popular beach, without any doubt, is Laginha Beach. Located behind the harbour, it is famous for its relaxed vibe, cocktail bars and amazing, turquoise-colored waters. In the early morning, people love to come here to walk or just stand in the water and talk to each other about the latest gossip.

Some of the best beaches are:

- *Sao Pedro Beach* (for watersport lovers)
- *Salamansa Bay* (for lonely walks)
- *Praia Grande* (for scenic walks, dangerous to swim though, great to be combined with a lunch in Calhau)

6.1.9. DO A DAY TRIP TO SANTO ANTAO

In my humble opinion, a day trip from Sao Vicente to Santo Antao is an absolute must! Even if you make it just one day, you should definitely visit the most impressive Cape Verdean Island! For me, Santo Antao is the best island in Cape Verde for hiking holidays! I recommend spending at least two days in Santo Antao.

Nowadays, there are three ferries per day connecting Sao Vicente to Santo Antao. Once you arrive in Porto Novo (the harbor of Santo Antao), you can start an island tour to the best places in Santo Antao.

If you have some time left, make sure to do at least one of the best hikes in Santo Antao!

As one day in Santo Antao may be extremely short, I recommend booking a guided day trip from Sao Vicente to Santo Antao.

6.1.10. VISIT TORRE DE BELEM

Did you know that Mindelo boasts a mini-replica of the *Torre de Belem* in Lisboa? I found this to be one of the most curious attractions in Mindelo!

The main difference between the *Torre de Belem* in Mindelo and the one in Lisbon is that first, the entrance is free. Second, the building hosts a very interesting exhibition about whaling in Cape Verde. I absolutely loved learning more about this tradition as it had a massive impact on Cape Verde's society, emigration, and culture.

Considered one of the best things to do in Sao Vicente, the *Torre de Belem* offers lovely views over the harbor of Mindelo and the colorful fishing boats in the bay.

6.1.11. VISIT THE LOCAL MARKETS

Visiting local markets is one of my favorite things to do in Cape Verde! No matter on which island I am, I always watch out for the market as it is the best place to mingle and soak up the local vibe.

Thankfully, there are several markets in Sao Vicente and more specifically in Mindelo. That means that you will have plenty of things to visit and to photograph. In case you want to buy stuff on the local markets, you always can (and even should!) negotiate the price if it seems too high for you! If not, let it be and be happy to support the local economy.

I tended to go always to the same places, as people started knowing me and gave me immediately the correct price. However, when you are a newbie in town, make sure that you do not pay double the price!

Some of the best markets are:

- *Fish Market* (Mindelo)
- *Old Market* (Avenida, Mindelo)
- *Praça Estrela* (Mindelo)

6.1.12. VISIT THE SMALL, INDEPENDENT SHOPS AND BARS IN MINDELO

Do you want to see the fewer know parts of Mindelo, but you find it hard to find small, independent shops?

I had the same issue when I was in Mindelo. The non-international shops seemed really hidden and secluded. It took me more than one month to get familiar with them and find the best small shops in Sao Vicente!

Visiting small shops is a great way of supporting the local community! That is why I strongly recommend spending some of your money here. On top, you will get a unique souvenir from Cape Verde as they boast a large offer of goods.

Some of the best small, independent shops in Mindelo are:

- *Lucy's* (Mindelo)
- *Trapos Polibel* (Mindelo)
- *Swell d'Sul* (Mindelo)
- *Capverdesign+Artesanato* (Mindelo)
- *Atelier de Violao Aniceto Gomes* (Mindelo)

6.2.   SANTIAGO

Santiago, Cape Verde's largest island is a surprising place where African traditions blend with the Portuguese ones in perfect harmony.

Located in the south of the country, off the West African coast, this patch of land is home to over half of Cape Verde's population and the main tourist hub.

It is known for its beaches and unique colonial towns, as well as its rich history and natural beauty. Unlike the other islands, which are characterized by slower paces, Santiago boasts it all.

From the bustling city life in Praia to the slower rhythms in Cidade Velha or the postcard-perfect Serra Malagueta National Park, you can find everything in Santiago!

Despite being packed with landmarks and places to see, Santiago is relatively concentrated.

How to get there:

Santiago is relatively easy to reach.

By plane: There are no direct flights from the USA but many European companies operate international flights from all the main airports in the USA as well as direct flights from some European cities to Praia.

The domestic flights from Fogo, Maio, Sal and Sao Vicente not only make it easy to get to Santiago from another island but also make island hopping quicker and more comfortable.

By boat: With a ferry from Brava and Fogo. While the ferry ride will take a while, it will give you the opportunity of admiring the unique archipelago from the sea.

How to get around:

Santiago does not have a well-established public transport. The easiest way to get around is with a rented car or motorcycle.

Thanks to the rapid growth of the island, many international car rental companies have offices at Praia International Airport.

Small motorcycle and quad rental shops are also established in Santiago. Provided you are in good shape, you could also rent a bike to tour the main landmarks but please always make sure to get your travel insurance upfront!

At the same time, *aluguer* (public taxis) provide quick connections between the various municipalities.

Where to stay:

Budget

    Pensao Esplanada Music Mito Alves

    Morabeza Kriol Hostel

Mid-Range

    Hotel Cesaria ***

    Kelly GuestHouse (outstanding, homemade breakfast!)

    Sol Hotel ***

Family-Friendly

    Pestana Tropico ****

    OASIS Praiamar ****

Beach-time

    King Fisher Village (Tarrafal)

    Kama Ku Café – Pousada and B&B (Cidade Velha)

Luxury

Pestana Tropico ****

Hotel Peróla ****

Hotel VIP Praia ****
OASIS Praiamar **** (top breakfast!)

---

1. VISIT PRAIA

The most important town on Santiago, Praia is also the capital of Cape Verde and its main tourist hub.

Founded in the 17th century, you can still admire the Portuguese influences in the beautiful colonial buildings.

Perhaps the liveliest city in Cape Verde, Praia is a world of contrasts! Undeniably, the best place to start exploring Praia is Sucupira.

This colorful African market has everything; from baked goods to fresh fruits and vegetables, clothes, toys, street food, and even livestock.

From here, head to the Plateau, Praia's oldest neighborhood. A busy place that gathers crowds of locals and tourists alike. All it takes to turn from chaos to a relaxing experience is to reach the viewpoint near the Presidential Palace.

A stroll by the seashore along the beach of Quebra Canela can fill you with energy for the night. Nightlife is bustling in Praia! Entertainment and food go hand in hand here, with most bars serving delicious dishes too.

One of the best places to go for both food and drinks is *Kebra Cabana*, a hipster bar serving excellent cocktails, burgers and grilled seafood. You can also enjoy live music each Friday night.

THINGS TO DO IN PRAIA, CAPE VERDE

Being the capital of Cape Verde and the largest city in the whole archipelago, Praia is the nation's main tourist hub. Yet, this lively place has managed to maintain its origins intact.

Touristy but not "that" touristy, it is an excellent choice for those who want to experience the authentic Cape Verdean culture without giving up modern comfort and amenities.

"Praia" means "beach" in Portuguese, a name inspired by the city's coastal nature. Here, you'll find amazing beaches of Cape Verde, a buzzing nightlife, as well as the slow paces characteristic to West Africa's colonial towns.

With dozens of landmarks as well as many hidden gems, Praia is an amazing destination. Don't take my word for granted but check out the fantastic things to do in Praia, Cape Verde, to see why this place should be at the top of your travel bucket list.

How to get to Praia

By flight: to international Praia airport, Cape Verde or with domestic flights from any Cape Verde Island

By boat: from any Cape Verde Island

Best Hotels in Praia, Cape Verde

Budget

Pensao Esplanada Music Mito Alves
Morabeza Kriol Hostel

Mid-Range

Hotel Cesaria ***
Kelly GuestHouse (*outstanding, home-made breakfast!*)
Sol Hotel ***
Pousada Praia Maria ***

Family-Friendly

Pestana Tropico ****
OASIS Praiamar ****

Luxury

Pestana Tropico ****
Hotel Peróla ****
Hotel Vip Praia ****
OASIS Praiamar **** (top breakfast!)

1. SHOP AT SUCUPIRA MARKET

Located in the heart of the city, the Sucupira market is undoubtedly Praia's most famous landmark. A visit here means immersing yourself completely into the colorful West African culture while discovering the authentic Cape Verdean lifestyle.

This semi-covered market sells a wide range of goods, from fresh produce like fruits and vegetables, to traditional clothes, bags, artisan objects, and local musical instruments.

Not only is this a great place for souvenir shopping, but it's also the best place for trying some delicious Cape Verdean Street food.

Opening times: Mon-Sun; 08.00-18.00

2. EXPLORE THE PLATEAU DISTRICT

Perhaps the most captivating part of the city, the *Plateau* district is the best place to visit for an afternoon stroll. Its suggestive name is given by the wide *plateau* on which it is located, overlooking the ocean and the port of Praia.

This is the historical center of the city, and here you can admire the Presidential Palace, the city hall and cathedral, or visit the

Ethnographic Museum to learn about the Cape Verdean culture and traditions. – Check guided tours here

3. HANG OUT AT QUEBRA CANELA BEACH

Located southwest of the city center, Quebra Canela beach is the epicenter of summer fun in Praia, Cape Verde. And it's the prettiest part of Praia's old town!

This expanse of black volcanic sand, sheltered by cliffs and bathed by the crystalline waters of the ocean, is a privileged space for a variety of water sports, from swimming and snorkeling to windsurfing and kayaking.

Sunbathing is another popular activity to do, while a few stylish beach bars offer a wide variety of snacks and drinks.

Praia boasts warm temperatures almost all-year-round. This makes it perfect for your Cape Verde winter holidays.

4. HAVE LUNCH IN ALEXANDRE ALBUQUERQUE SQUARE

If you like history, the Praça Alexandre Albuquerque Square is an unmissable landmark in Praia.

Located in the southwestern side of the Plateau, it's lined with beautiful colonial houses, while the public park in the center of the square is a true oasis for relaxation.

After admiring the buildings and strolling through the park, the best thing to do here is to enjoy the bustling rhythms of the capital city of Cape Verde while having a tasty lunch in one of the many nearby bars. For me, it is one of the best things to do in Cape Verde.

5. HAVE A CAIPIRINHA AT PRAINHA BEACH

Situated on the coast, south of the city center, Prainha beach attracts locals and tourists alike. Surrounded by some of the best hotels in Praia, Cape Verde, Prainha beach is popular among surfers, divers, snorkelers, as well as families with kids.

Besides usual beach activities, this place is also known for the amazing beach parties thrown by the nearby restaurants and bars. Thus, this is the perfect place for tasting caipirinha in Cape Verde.

What makes this cocktail special is the fact that in Vape Verde, it's made with grogue instead of cachaça. Moreover, you can also try many alternative recipes with mango, papaya, or other tropical fruits instead of the traditional lime.

6. GO SHOPPING FOR ARTISAN SOUVENIRS

Things to do in Praia, Cape Verde, Cape Verde is known for its pottery, but traditional clothes, bags, and jewelry are other popular options.

Souvenir shopping is by far one of the best things to do in Praia, especially if this is your first time visiting West Africa. And by far, the best souvenirs to shop are the local artisan ones.

Cape Verde is known for its pottery, but traditional clothes, bags, and jewelry are other popular options.

The best place for artisan souvenir shopping in Praia is the Sucupira Market or the Main Market on the *Plateau*. Alternatively, the *Praia Shopping* is a modern shopping mall where you can find both conventional and traditional shops.

The main street of Praia on the *Plateau* also boasts several souvenir shops selling products made in Cape Verde.

7. LEARN ABOUT HISTORY IN MUSEUM AMILCAR CABRAL

Santiago, Cape Verde, has the richest history in the archipelago. The first Europeans coming to colonize Cape Verde arrived here first, not to mention the horrific slave trade that took place on the island.

It is essential to learn more about the history of this place if you want to fully understand the Cape Verdean culture, and the best place to do so is the small but impressive *Amilcar Cabral Museum*.

Dedicated to preserving the memory of the revolutionary *Amilcar Cabral*, the museum hosts a collection of photographs and other memorabilia about *Cabral*'s fight for freedom from colonialism.

Opening times: Hours vary. It is recommended to book your visit in advance.

8. ENJOY CAPE VERDEAN MUSIC

Cape Verde is renowned for many things, and music is one of them. Traditional sounds vary from *morna* and *coladeira* to *batuko* and *funaná*, and the best thing is that many places across the town organize traditional live music nights.

Of all, the *Quintal da Música – 5al da Música* and the *Kebra Cabana* are the most renowned. The former is located next to Quebra Canela beach, a place where you can enjoy live music nights each Friday, as well as exquisite snacks or full meals. The latter is a great place to hit if you want to listen to some of the best *funaná* Cape Verde music.

Other Cape Verde music styles you cannot miss are morna, coladeira, and batuca.

9. INDULGE IN LOCAL FOOD AND DRINKS

From all towns across the islands of the archipelago, Praia is perhaps your best bet when it comes to tasting delicious Cape Verde foods.

The local dishes vary from light seafood platters and salads to hearty meals, including the exquisite cachupa stew.

In the city center, the *90 (Noventa) Bistro* is a popular stop for tourists and locals alike. The restaurant serves both local and international dishes, while the atmosphere here is super-friendly and relaxing.

The *Churrasqueira Dragoeiro* is a restaurant, popular for its charcoal-grilled tuna and chicken, as well as its succulent pork skewers.

Seafood lovers can indulge in some local specialties at the *Cafe Sofia – Copacabana Bar & Lounge Praia*, a restaurant popular for its grilled shrimps and marinated octopus.

Some of the best places to eat in Praia are:

- Kasa Katxupa – For breakfast and revisited, traditional food
- Linha D'agua – Next to Prainha beach, great beach vibes
- O Poeta – Sophisticated seafood and great views
- Beramar Grill – Best seafood according to locals
- Pao Quente – Portuguese Style pastry shop
- Nhamii Ice Creams – Great home-made ice creams!
- Tambake – Great vegan and vegetarian food
- D Concept Design Store – Revisited traditional food with Portuguese influences

10. DO A GRAFFITI TOUR

With graffiti slowly transforming into an accepted form of urban art, more and more local tour operators in Praia now propose exciting "graffiti tours".

Not only such a tour will give you the opportunity to have unique insights into Praia's history, but your guide will also show you some of the city's hidden gems and sights.

11. DO A CITY TOUR WITH A LOCAL GUIDE

Undeniably, the best way to discover a new place is with the help of a local guide, especially if you only have limited time.

Indeed, hiring a Cape Verde guide is your best bet if you don't want to miss any of the important landmarks of the city during a short stay.

Most Praia city tours start with a stroll along the Alexandre Albuquerque square to admire the Presidential Palace, the city hall and the colonial houses and then continue with shopping at the Sucupira Market.

Along the way, your guide will also share with you some unique insights and historical facts that will surprise you about Praia, Cape Verde.

12. VISIT PRAIA DO SAO FRANCISCO

A visit to Praia do Sao Francisco is a must if you love remote beaches.

It is a very nice sandy beach, at 15/20 mins driving from Praia. It comes with a second smaller beach when passing the rocks. Much parking space is available, and it is a great place to snorkel (if the visibility allows).

2. LEARN ABOUT THE PAST IN CIDADE VELHA

The first capital of the archipelago and the birthplace of the Cape Verdean culture, Cidade Velha is also a UNESCO heritage site and a place you cannot miss if you want to learn more about the country's history and culture.

Meaning "Old Town" in English, Cidade Velha brags with over 500 years of history.

It was the first European settlement in the tropics, as well as one of the most important places in the world for the slave trade. Its beautiful historic center still bears signs of the colonial-style architecture.

Undeniably, the best thing to do here is to stroll along its characteristic streets and admire its gorgeous colonial houses, typically along with Rua Banana or Rua Carreira.

3. EXPLORE THE REAL FORTE DE SÃO FILIPE

Located in Cidade Velha, the *Forte Real de São Filipe* is an impressive 16th-century fortress that overlooks the entire area of Ribeira Grande, Cidade Velha's original name.

It served as a defense system for centuries but today, it attracts visitors with sweeping views over the town and surroundings. No doubt, this is the perfect place to take that Insta-worthy shot while visiting Santiago!

4. VISIT THE MARKET OF ASSOMADA

Assomada is a quaint little town located a 45 min drive northwest from Praia. Counting around 15.000 inhabitants, though, it is the second-largest municipality on the island. It is essential on any Santiago tour!

Impressing with a pleasant combination of urban and countryside areas, this town is also an important commercial center, and famous for its colorful market.

Undeniably, this is the best place to visit if you want to immerse yourself in the authentic African culture.

Founded in 1931, the market of Assomada is the largest of Santiago. Besides a wide variety of fresh local products, it is also the perfect place for souvenir shopping if you want to go home with an original handcrafted object.

Once you have explored the market, do not forget to visit the *Norberto Tavares* cultural center, a cultural space, and a museum dedicated to the famous Cape Verdean musician.

Housed in the former post office, the center was established in 2008, when the popular *Museu da Tabanca* was moved from Assomada to Chã de Tanque.

5. GO HIKING IN SERRA MALAGUETA

Home to important threatened and endemic species, Serra Malagueta is a real paradise for hikers! This splendid natural park is not only the most important ecological area on the island, but it also encompasses beautiful landscapes and impresses with a vast network of trails that cross lush forests.

From all, Ribeira Principal is undeniably the most spectacular! Covering the entire area from the park's entrance to the ocean, it leads you to the discovery of a wide variety of landscapes.

Undoubtedly, an experience to live if you want to see more than only colonial towns and beaches during your trip.

6. CLIMB THE HIGHEST PEAK: PICO DA ANTONIA

If hiking is your thing, another place to explore is the protected *Parque Natural da Serra do Pico de Antania*. An important bird area and home to thick forests, the natural park is famous for its *Pico de Antónia*, the highest point of the island!

The views you can enjoy from 1.392 m above the sea level are spectacular, but you will need to be in shape to get there!

That said, the mountain is located close to Assomada. Therefore, if you do not feel like climbing, you can stroll through the market, and admire some views of the peak from afar.

7. VISIT THE TARRAFAL CONCENTRATION CAMP

Holidays in Santiago are often synonymous with relaxed sunbathing, hikes and watersports. Visiting the Tarrafal concentration camp, thus, might not be on your bucket list.

However, even if it is sometimes hard to uncover the darker chapters of human history, this peculiar prison deserves a visit.

Built-in 1933 by Portuguese dictator Antonio de Oliveira Salazar, this place housed political prisoners and Africans fighting against colonial rule.

Many of these prisoners were held here until 1975 when Cape Verde won its independence.

Despite being now turned into a museum that displays photos and artifacts from the time, the Tarrafal concentration camp still transudes the sadness of the horrors that happened between its walls.

While the Tarrafal concentration camp is a place for reflection, you can easily unwind and get back into vacation mode at Tarrafal Beach.

Located at the foot of Monte Graciosa, about one hour by car from Praia, this golden sand beach is a paradise for surfers, snorkelers and divers!

The best thing about this beach is that it is never overcrowded. The only downside is the lack of amenities, such as beach chairs and umbrellas, but you can relax after sunbathing in one of the many restaurants or bars nearby.

9. VISIT A POTTERY NEAR TARRAFAL

Cape Verde offers much more than pristine scenery and days by the sea. Unique traditions and crafts include the art of pottery, and you can join a workshop if you want to.

Located in the rural zone of Tarrafal behind Monte Graciosa, the *Trás di Munti* pottery center is a great place to visit by yourself or with children.

10. VISIT THE RABELADOS IN ESPINHO BRANCO

If you love discovering new cultures, visiting the *Rabelados* in Espinho Branco is essential! This unique religious community was formed in the 1940s by a group of locals who rebelled against the liturgical reforms introduced by the Catholic Church.

Today, the largest community of "rebels" lives in Espinho Branco, a small village on the northern side of the island. They are mainly involved in agriculture, handicrafts, and fishing.

Living in semi-isolated conditions, they maintained their own culture and traditions based on a closer relationship with the land and nature. Their religious rituals are unique, and you can attend ceremonies on Saturdays and Sundays.

They have a small shop where you can purchase hand-made souvenirs and support the local community.

11. DO AN ISLAND TOUR

Santiago might be the largest of the Cape Verde islands, but the truth is that it is still compact. If you only have one day to spend here, an island tour is your best bet.

Numerous companies offer group or private tours, or you could simply rent a car, and create your own route. To have a glimpse of the authentic lifestyle, though, hiring a local guide is essential!

Typical tours include a drive around the Natural Park of Serra Malagueta, a few hours of strolling through characteristic neighborhoods in Praia, sunbathing at Tarrafal Beach, as well as visits at the Assomada market and the *Rabelados* community.

Most experiences also include a traditional lunch with a Cape Verdean family, usually consisting of the conventional *cuscus* (couscous) and *fidjos*.

12. STAY IN AN ECOLODGE

Accommodation can make or break the deal when planning a holiday! If you love immersing yourself in the local culture, the ecolodge might be your best bet when visiting Santiago

Quinta da Montanha is a unique place, nestled in a remote area in the heart of the Norte National Park.

Instead of a crowded, touristy hotel, you will discover a place focused on a sustainable lifestyle. Indeed, Quinta da Montanha transudes the eco-friendly philosophy of its warm-hearted owners.

Not only is this a perfect place for casual travelers looking for a unique lodging, but it is also a great choice if you want to spend a few days away from the modern hustle and bustle.

Offering half or full board in its restaurant and bar, quick access to the beach, as well as lots of space to soak up the sun, this place attracts those who need the utmost relaxation.

13. ENJOY THE LOCAL FOOD

Finally, yet importantly, one of the coolest things to do in Santiago is trying the local cuisine!

Some of the must-tries include *cachupa,* a slow cooked stew of corn, beans, cassava, sweet potato, fish or meat.

Cuscus (couscous), *moreia* (fried eel) and *buzio* are other delicious dishes that you should try! The island is known for its exquisite seafood and fish dishes.

Restaurante Maracuja in Tarrafal is one of the best eateries in Santiago. From fresh food dishes to traditional ones, you will be spoilt with choices, and will taste some of the most amazing food in Cape Verde!

90 (Noventa) Bistro in Praia awaits you with loads of traditional dishes, including local goat cheese, cuscus, vegetable stews, as well as seafood.

For dinner with a view, *Kebra Cabana* can surely satisfy even the most demanding tourists. Located next to Quebra Canela Beach, it is an excellent choice for lunch or dinner after exploring this beautiful district.

In the Prainha district, you can find the *Creole – Food and Arts Restaurant*. A landmark for tourists and locals wanting to taste African, Cajun and Creole dishes, it surprises with a unique atmosphere and high-class services. While it may maybe cost a bit more than the average restaurant in Praia, a dinner here will surely be the highlight of your holiday in Santiago!

14. DO A DAY TRIP TO MAIO

The easternmost island in the archipelago, Maio is Cape Verde's best-kept secret. This hidden paradise was initially colonized for the exploitation of its salt, and it now impresses with quaint rhythms of life.

A day trip from Praia to Maio will allow you to discover another face of Cape Verde's history, culture and traditions, not to mention the possibility to enjoy pristine beaches and breathtaking scenery, as well as discover Cape Verde's largest forest, mainly composed of acacia trees.

Even though Cape Verde is so much more than beautiful beaches, I wanted to dedicate a section on the best beaches in Cape Verde. After all, most people think of stunning pristine beaches when they think of Cape Verde.

However, when going to the beach, please be careful, as the currents can be extremely strong, even though the water looks calm on the surface! I always recommend getting information from the locals! Wherever I can, I share precaution tips for each recommended beach in in this guide.

SANTA MARIA BEACH

Santa Maria Beach in Sal is probably one of the most famous beaches in Cape Verde. No wonder with those clear, turquoise waters and fine golden sand! On top, you will have plenty of activities to do.

It is located south of the island and is the main beach of Santa Maria, which is the main tourist hub of Sal. It is here where you will find all the luxury resorts and best hotels.

There are countless beach bars and restaurants. Thus, it is the perfect place to unwind and enjoy. As it is the most popular beach, expect to find quite a lot of people and tourists during high season!

The water is calm and perfect to swim. I also enjoyed it for a long walk on the pier where the fishermen sell the catch of the day.

Santa Maria Beach is a real must during your holidays in Sal!

PONTA PRETA BEACH (BLACK BEACH)

Ponta Preta Beach, close to Santa Maria, is like the quiet and more natural version of Santa Maria Beach. It is located southwest of the island.

Located right next to the famous Santa Maria Beach, Ponta Preta Beach (also known as "Black Beach") is much more tranquil and perfect for long walks on the beach.

It is also a popular spot for turtle watching!

The landscape of Ponta Preta Beach is much more natural and unspoiled. There are almost no resorts, nor restaurants! Occasionally a sailing boat or a kitesurfer passes by. Otherwise, it is just you and the sound of the waves!

KITE BEACH

Kite Beach is the best beach in Cape Verde for watersport and kitesurf lovers! Either you can reach it by a 20 min walk from Santa Maria or you take an *aluguer* (collective taxi).

Thanks to the wind and the impressive waves, it is considered one of the best beaches for kitesurfing in the world! Already from far, you can spot hundreds of colorful kites flying around.

However, Kite Beach is nothing for those who want to spend a relaxing day on the beach! It is super windy! However, if you want to take a kitesurf lesson, this is the place to be!

With a little bit of luck, your instructor will be a kitesurfing world champion. You will be able to train with the best of the best!

BIKINI BEACH CLUB

The *Bikini Beach Club* in Santa Maria is one of the top attractions in Sal!

Located only a short walk from Santa Maria Beach, you will find it just in front of the *Tortuga Beach Hotel*.

It was built "into" the sea and can be accessed by a scenic pier. It is the best place to spend a day on the ocean but in a more luxurious way. You can rent sun loungers, enjoy the Jacuzzi and swimming pool, and have exclusive cocktails.

It also organizes many events that are the perfect occasion to dance until the sun rises! The Bikini Beach Club is a real must when you are in Sal!

7.2. BEST BEACHES IN BOA VISTA

SANTA MONICA BEACH

Santa Monica Beach is a real paradise beach! It stretches for more than 10 km on the south-west of the island. It is all about white, light yellow sand and turquoise water!

It is so vast and sometimes you will feel like you have the entire ocean and beach for yourself! During the season, you can even spot whales!

Santa Monica Beach is thus perfect for long walks along the beach. However, please be careful with swimming as the tides can be strong! As it is quite offbeat, better bring water and some snacks along! There is almost no shade, so I recommend taking a hat and sunscreen.

There are still no large resorts, so you will be privileged to enjoy this beautiful place. However, please remember though to be respectful to Mother Nature!

PRAIA DE CHAVES

Praia de Chaves is one of the most popular places for kitesurfing in Boa Vista. This beach is about 5 km long and is very coveted for long beach walks. There are some resorts close to Rabil. They figure among the top hotels in Cape Verde. The rest is still unspoiled.

The resorts located on Praia de Chaves are the *Iberostar Club Boa Vista* and the *Royal Horizons Boa Vista*.

There is also a kitesurf school for those who want to take their first lessons. Sometimes the wind and sea can be rough though! Thus, please always be careful before going for a swim!

PRAIA DE ATALANTA WITH ITS SHIPWRECK

Praia de Atalanta and Costa da Boa Esperança are located in the north of the island. Praia de Atalanta is one of the most important places to visit in Boa Vista as it is home to the most famous shipwreck of the Cape Verde islands!

Indeed, this old Spanish cargo ship ran aground in the 1960s and became a popular photo motive for tourists. Much of the boat has fallen apart since the 1960s and eventually, it will completely disappear! Thus, be quick to visit!

Praia de Atalanta is vast, and the sea can be rough sometimes! I also heard of some armed robberies that happened on this beach so please watch out!

PRAIA DE CABRAL / PRAIA DE CRUZ

Praia de Cabral, also known as "Praia de Cruz", is the beach of the capital, Sal Rei. It is tiny in comparison with the other beaches of Boa Vista. However, even as a capital, Sal Rei only has the size of a village! Thus, it has this characteristic "No stress" vibe.

However, you will have all the facilities if you are looking for a perfect day on the beach. Many beach bars offer shade and refreshing drinks.

From here, you can also walk to the nearby *Capela de Nossa Senhora de Fátima.*

7.3. BEST BEACHES IN MAIO

Maio is is my favorite island when it comes to the best beaches!

Maio can be compared to Sal or Boa Vista before they were "discovered" and exploited by large resorts, and invaded by the tourist masses. Consequently, Maio has the most laid-back feeling and the pristine beaches.

Being one of the least visited islands of Cape Verde, you will mostly share the vast beaches only with the local community, which is the most warm-hearted ever!

BITXE ROCHA

Bitche Rocha is the main beach of Vila do Maio (also known as "Porto Ingles"). It is here where the colorful fishermen's ships arrive. It is clean, safe to swim here and a fabulous place for people watching!

From Bitche Rocha, you will spot the pier, which will eventually become a big harbor one day! Behind the pier, you will have the most beautiful beach I have ever seen! It is huge, vast and completely empty!

However, please do not swim here! The tides can be dangerous and the winds quite strong! I consider the beach behind the pier of Maio one of my "happy places" on this planet!

PRAIONA

This is probably the best beach of Maio! According *Bemvindo* (my guide), it is his favorite beach as well. It is easy to see why: it is vast and empty, the sand is so fine, the waters are turquoise, you have views on the hills of Maio and on top, and it is safe to swim!

Also known as "Praia Gonçalo", the beach is located close to Pedro Vaz and Pilao Cao. There are no food stalls here, so make sure to bring water, some snacks, and sunscreen of course!

You had better reach the Praiona with a 4×4 vehicle or with a guided tour.

RIBEIRA DOM JOAO BEACH

Ribeira Dom João has one of the largest populations of Maio after Porto Ingles. It is famous for its cheese factory managed by women from the local community. Make sure to stop here and fuel up on goat cheese! It is on the way to the beach and a great way to connect with the local community!

After crossing Ribeira Dom Joao and circumventing the palm oasis, you will reach the coast. The "road" finishes on top of a cliff from which you will enjoy spectacular views on the beaches of Ribeira Dom Joao.

Make your way down to the beach and be ready to spend an unforgettable day on the beach. In addition, here, please be aware of the tides and the wind!

According to a local, this beach is coveted among surfers (even though there are not many that make their way to Maio).

SANTANA BEACH

Santana Beach is located next to Morrinho, in the northwest of the island.

It is a coveted spot to watch turtles! Other beaches to observe turtles nestling are Praia Real and Ponta Preta.

LAGINHA BEACH

Laginha Beach is to Mindelo what Copacabana is to Rio de Janeiro! It is the home beach of Mindelo, Cape Verde's cultural capital, famous for its music and artists.

The beach can be reached within a 10 min walk from the city center. It is not very large but it has the most crystal-clear turquoise waters on the island, and the sand is very fine and golden!

Recently, a beach bar opened up serving refreshing drinks and tasty snacks. It is the perfect place to spend a day on the beach and watch the daily grind of Mindelo.

Laginha Beach is safe for swimmers and protected from the wind. If you are lucky, you will even assist one of the events that are sometimes held on the beach! I do not recommend visiting Laginha Beach at night, as it might be dangerous!

SAO PEDRO BEACH

Sao Pedro Beach is the best beach in Sao Vicente for windsurfers. Located only a few minutes behind the airport, this beach is quite windy and has strong tides! Thus, I do not recommend swimming here!

There is a windsurfing school where you can rent windsurf material and take lessons. There are also a few apartments in construction and the *Foya Branca Hotel* has a lovely terrace to enjoy views on the beach.

It is great to visit when you are up for a walk on the beach and want to enjoy the ambiance of a small fishermen village.

There is also a trail going to the lighthouse, which will provide you spectacular views on the coast. Take good walking shoes with you, as the path is sometimes quite steep!

You can get to Sao Pedro Beach by *aluguer* (collective taxi) from Mindelo to Sao Pedro.

PRAIA GRANDE

Praia Grande Beach is one of my favorite beaches in Sao Vicente! It is located on the east of the island, in the bay between Bahia das Gatas and Calhau.

It is huge and the views on the coast and the mountains of Sao Vicente make this one a real paradise beach!

In addition, here the tides are strong and when I visited, there were quite big waves! Therefore, it is not for swimming but rather for playing in the waves!

After walking on the beach, and playing with the waves for endless hours, I recommend heading to Calhau (about a 15 min walk) and have lunch in one of the restaurants that are famous for their seafood.

I recommend *Restaurant Hamburg* (they prepare their seafood on the barbecue!), *Chez Loutcha* or *Tony do Calhau*. All those places are quite popular on Sundays!

You can reach Praia Grande with an *aluguer* (collective taxi) from Mindelo to Calhau. However, please be aware that by night, there are fewer *aluguers* (collective taxis) going back to Mindelo!

Santo Antao is not really known as being a top beach destination. Thanks to its mountains and dramatic valleys, created many years ago by volcanic eruptions, Santo Antao became a paradise for hikers and outdoor lovers! It is one of my favorite places to hike and the mountainous landscape simply left me speechless! It is very easy to fall in love with Santo Antao!

If after all that walking, you want to spend some time on the beach, you need to be prepared to make some efforts to get there!

Santo Antao does not really have beaches and it is dangerous to swim in places that are not marked as proper beaches! Almost every year, tourists die because they wanted to refresh

225

themselves during a hike! The tide carried them away! So, please do not!

However, a few beaches on Santo Antao allow you to spend a lovely day on the beach.

TARRAFAL BEACH

Tarrafal Beach is probably the most famous beach of Santo Antao. It is located on the southwest of Santo Antao, whereas the most spectacular hikes are all located in the northwest of the island.

Monte Trigo de Tarrafal, and its adjacent beach, mainly consists of fishermen, and until recently, they had no electricity! Nowadays, you can find a few shops and bars.

Tarrafal Beach is characterized by its laid-back atmosphere and beautiful views on the rocky coast. If you are lucky, you will even spot a whale or a turtle!

Tarrafal is usually very quiet and thus perfect for a swim! However, always trust your gut! As it is very tempting to stay longer in Tarrafal, you should have a look at the few guesthouses!

Otherwise, you can easily reach Tarrafal by *aluguer* (collective taxi) from Porto Novo or even by hiking.

PRAIA DO TOPO

Praia do Topo is located just outside Porto Novo, which is the village where the ferry from Sao Vicente arrives.

The beach has beautiful views on the rocky coast of Santo Antao and is perfect to enjoy some rest before heading to the north of Santo Antao and enjoy the hikes.

The ambiance is laid-back and as the beach is protected from the winds, you will enjoy swimming here!

PONTA DO SOL BEACH

Finally, there are also a few beaches in the north of Santo Antao! This are good news, as the best hikes of Santo Antao are all located in the north. Some of the most famous trails of Santo Antao are Cova – *Paul Valley*, *Ponta do Sol – Fontainhas – Cha d'Igreja*, and *Xoxo*.

Ponta do Sol has one of the largest populations on Santo Antao and can be seen as the main tourist hub on the island. Here, you will find a beautiful town center, many bars, shops, and a lively local community.

There are two places to swim in Ponta do Sol. You can refresh yourself where the fishermen boats arrive or you can opt to visit the beach of Ponta do Sol that can only be reached by hiking a rather dangerous trail, or by asking fishermen to take you.

This beach is called "Praia de Lisboa" and is one of the only beaches in northern Santo Antao.

Please do not go for a swim on the beaches during the hike from Ponta do Sol to Cha d'Igreja! It is here where already several tourists have died due to the strong tides!

NATURAL SWIMMING POOLS IN SINAGOGA

The natural swimming pools in Sinagoga are some of my favorite places to swim in northern Santo Antao. There is also a large beach close to it. However, the tides are too strong to swim there! It is actually something only for advanced surfers!

Luckily, there are the natural swimming pools that are protected from waves and winds! They are very enjoyable, and offer fabulous views on the mountains of Santo Antao!

They can be reached when you come from Ribeira Grande to Sinagoga. Right after the tunnel, you turn left and walk down the coast. There is a little *mercearia* (grocery) in Sinagoga where you can stock up on snacks and drinks.

The name of the village comes from a Jewish community that left Portugal and found a new home in Santo Antão. Nowadays, you can still see the impressive ruins of the synagogue, which are right next to the natural swimming pools.

After the Jewish community extinguished, the building was used as a sanatorium to help leprosy patients. Despite the macabre historical background, the ruins are a great photo motive, and the swimming pools are a lovely place to visit!

7.6. BEST BEACHES IN SANTIAGO

I tend to say that Santiago is for the undecided ones. It has the city life in Praia, important attractions in Cidade Velha for history buffs, mountains to hike and gorgeous beaches to hang out.

TARRAFAL BEACH

Located in the north of Santiago, Tarrafal Beach is without any doubt one of the best beaches of Santiago! It is adjacent to the green Monte Graciosa and Tarrafal. Only a few years ago, Tarrafal was not touristy at all! Now, more and more visitors come to Tarrafal in order to enjoy the beauty of its beach.

Another reason to visit Tarrafal is its museum about the political prisoners held in the Tarrafal concentration camp between 1936 and 1974.

Tarrafal Beach is pure bliss thanks to its soft sand, clear waters and amenities! It is safe to swim and it is a popular destination for family travelers too.

As Tarrafal is one of the most popular getaways in Santiago, please be aware at night from muggers!

QUEBRA CANELA BEACH

Quebra Canela Beach is one of the larger beaches of Praia. Located southwest of the city center, it is not too big, has fine sands and even a restaurant! During weekends, it can become quite crowded!

Some readers complained about the litter at Quebra Canela!

PRAINHA

Some describe Prainha Beach as the most picturesque beach of Praia! Located at a short walk from the city center, this beach is small but has everything it takes to have a fabulous day at the beach!

Authorities are making efforts to keep the beach clean and consequently, it got quite popular! It is nowadays a fabulous place for families! As the water is calm, you can go for a swim.

There are a few bars, but no shade at all!

PRAIA DO SAO FRANCISCO

A visit to Praia do Sao Francisco is a must if you love remote beaches.

It is a very nice sandy beach, about 15/20 mins driving from Praia. It comes with a second smaller beach when passing the rocks. Much parking space is available and it is a great place to snorkel (if the visibility allows).

7.7. BEST BEACHES IN BRAVA & FOGO

Brava is one of the smallest inhabited islands in Cape Verde. It is popular among hikers and trekkers due to its mountainous landscape. However, that does not mean that you need to renounce on a refreshing bath!

There are not many beaches on Brava, but the island probably boasts some of the prettiest natural swimming pools of Cape Verde. They can be found in Faja d'Agua and provide lovely views on the rocky coast of Brava.

You can easily spend the entire day here and enjoy the swimming pools in all their beauty!

There are no facilities but I highly recommend having lunch in Faja d'Agua and having a look at the desert airport of Brava which is a short walk away from the swimming pools.

BRAVA: PRAIA PORTO DE FURNA

Praia Porto de Furna is located in Furna. It is one of the only natural beaches in Brava. It is certainly not the best one to swim, as the ferry from Fogo arrives here, and it is the place where the fishermen set out to sea!

However, Praia Porto de Furna is a lovely place for people watching! The sea around Brava can be rough so please be aware of the tides!

FOGO BEACH

Fogo has one of the most stunning attractions in Cape Verde: the volcano! Whereas the volcano is one of the top tourist attractions, a few beaches provide a welcome refreshment on the beach after hiking.

There is Praia da Bila beach that is located 40 m below Sao Filipe, the capital of Fogo. However, it can be sometimes dirty and the sea can be rough! Thus, be aware of the currents and tides!

An alternative to Praia da Bila is Porto de Vale de Cavaleiros. There is a small beach, which is cleaner, and the water is less rough.

8. SUSTAINABLE TRAVEL TIPS: SMALL, INDEPENDENT BUSINESSES

TOURISM IN CAPE VERDE: WHY YOU MATTER!

Cape Verde has extremely ambitious plans to become one of the most important holiday destinations in Western Africa.

So far, Sal and Boa Vista have been converted into mass tourism hubs with large all-inclusive resorts managed by the most important hotel groups. Unfortunately, the local population does not see much of the benefits generated by tourism on Sal and Boa Vista.

Even worse, the massive growth on these two islands fosters emigration from other, smaller islands. Hoping to get a (not ver rewarding) job in the tourism sector, young people leave the poorer islands such as Brava, Fogo and Santo Antao. The results are abandoned villages and lands.

However, in theory, there is no need to leave the peripherical islands of Cape Verde. Every single one is a treasure on its own and mostly, they differ a lot! Not only the landscapes, but also the people and the culture are very different on each island.

For some reasons (that are unknown to me yet), Sal and Boa Vista get all the attention of large tour operators and most tourists in general, leaving the other islands deserted.

The good news is though, that you can change this! Take the decision to go beyond Sal and Boa Vista and you will be rewarded with a travel experience of a lifetime! Go dance alone on the empty beaches of Maio, wonder at the mesmerizing valleys of Santo Antao, listen to century-old music in Mindelo, or be in awe of the Fogo volcano! In short, fall in love with the real wonders of Cape Verde!

WHY WE NEED TO THINK OF A DIFFERENT FORM OF HOLIDAYS

Most visitors that are looking to spend holidays in Cape Verde immediately think of Sal or Boa Vista.

However, there is so much more to see than the international, anonymous resorts in Sal or Boa Vista. Because, if you want it or not, supporting this kind of tourism in these two islands that are totally desert is doing no good to anybody!

There are several points that you need to keep in mind when you opt for beach holidays in Sal or Boa Vista:

- Besides some exceptions, most hotels are managed by foreigners or/and large hotel groups.

- Most resorts are all inclusive resorts, which means that the money stays within the resort. Tourists hardly leave their accommodation as everything has already been paid for. Thus, the local restaurants do not profit from tourism, as they should.

- Sal and Boa Vista are desert islands. It is surreal and revolting to see hotel fortresses with hundreds of hotel rooms and tourists taking endless showers! In some cases, the water of the local population is even being cut off so that the tourists can take their showers!

- Showing the wrong idea of the Cape Verdean culture. When I stayed in Sal, I noticed that the entertainment program of many hotels consisted of "local dance shows". I saw young girls and boys dancing in Tarzan costumes with leopard prints! First, Cape Verde is not Africa! Second, even if it was, in Africa, people do not wear Tarzan outfits! Cape Verde's culture is a unique mix of European and African influences. However, its cultural wealth is not shown at all in the anonymous resorts.

- The emigration. Young people from the poorer islands such as Fogo, Brava, Santo Antao and Maio are leaving their homes to work in Sal or Boa Vista for supposed better working conditions. The results are deserted landscapes and societies.

- The living conditions. Cape Verdeans have to pay extremely high rents to live in the backcountry of Sal or Boa Vista. As each single fruit, vegetable or any other product has to be imported; the cost of living is extremely expensive! The prices for fresh fruit are similar to the prices in Europe! That means that even if those people earn a little bit more money when they work for an international hotel group, they spend most of it in extremely expensive rents and living costs. On top, many of them are supposed to send money to their families on a regular basis.
- A threat to nature. Large hotels are often built on preserved beaches that boast rich biodiversity and are turtle nesting sites.

When thinking about it, you may wonder how this is even possible. In my humble and innocent opinion, I think that the lack of regulation is partly responsible. In Europe, this kind of tourism would never be allowed!

I guess that you can see now why it is so important to diversify tourism in Cape Verde. The good news is that it is very simple! You can change everything with your decision!

You may spend some days in Sal or Boa Vista but then, take a plane or a ferry and explore how different each island is. Explore the vertiginous valleys of Santo Antao, the natural wonder of Mount Fogo, the cultural scene of Mindelo, and the untouched beaches of Maio.

There are so many more things to do in Cape Verde than staying locked in a resort in Sal or Boa Vista!

WHAT TO DO TO SUPPORT SUSTAINABLE TOURISM

The first step is acknowledging that you can make the difference! However, it will cost a little effort. It means that you will need to go beyond the obvious, and question your purchases, dinners and hotels.

Unfortunately, in Cape Verde, local shops, restaurants and hotels managed by locals are often hard to find or to identify. Often, they are not featured on Booking, TripAdvisor or Viator.

These local businesses have been there long before the large hotel groups came and there was simply no need to invest or even think about marketing. On top, they often just cannot afford to pay high commissions to online platforms.

I discovered most of the places listed in this article by talking to locals and wandering around. Sometimes, you would not even know if you enter a private house or a shop, but you end up buying a fabulous t-shirt created by a local designer!

In fact, it is very hard to find small, independent businesses in Cape Verde. In order to facilitate the task, I listed for you every sustainable, local business I stumbled upon during my travels through Cape Verde.

The main criteria for being listed here as "sustainable" are:

- Businesses managed by the local community
- Showcasing the Cape Verdean culture
- Being as eco-friendly as possible
- Preserving Cape Verde's biodiversity

8.1. SUSTAINABLE HOLIDAYS IN SAL

Along with Boa Vista, Sal is one of the main hubs for mass tourism in Cape Verde. Most resorts concentrate in Santa Maria, located in the southern part of the island.

Logging prices have risen a lot so that locals are pushed out from Santa Maria and have to relocate to the interior towns like Espargos.

However, your actions can make a difference and make sure that the local community can profit more from tourism!

WHERE TO STAY

It can be hard to find sustainable hotel alternatives in Sal. Most accommodation options are large hotels, managed by international groups.

Thus, if you want to be on the sustainable side, I would recommend staying at smaller hotels, managed by local families. Even though you will maybe need to make a few compromises when it comes to comfort, I think that supporting a local family compensates for it all.

Sobrado Boutique Hotel ****

Residencial Cabo Verde Palace

Hotel Central Sal ***

Hotel Da Luz ***

Hotel Dunas de Sal ****

Odjo D'Agua Hotel ****

LOCAL SHOPS

- *Mercado Municipal* (on the main market in Santa Maria. I recommend looking for tailor-made dresses by the Senegalese tailors.)
- *Djunta Mo Art* (products made in Cape Verde)
- *Art Hands*
- *K.Kloset*

LOCAL RESTAURANTS

- *Cafe Criolo*
- *Nos Brinde*
- *Kverde*
- *Restaurante Bar d'Fogo*
- *Bar di Nos*

LOCAL GUIDES

- *Malu Turismo (maluturismo.comercial@gmail.com)*
- *Rotas Cruzadas (+2382422030)*
- *Morabitur Viagens e Turismo (+2382422070)*
- *Beni Teodoro Excursions & Transfer (+2389505161)*

HOW TO SUPPORT THE LOCAL CULTURE

It is well worth it to go out of your resort and walk in the streets behind the main boulevard of Santa Maria. It is here where you will still find some of the local, original daily grinds. However, even here, the Cape Verdean population is slowly moving out due to the rising logging prices.

Concerning restaurants, I usually eat where locals are sitting on the terrace. You can get a very tasty meal for as little as 5 €!

For shopping, I absolutely recommend heading to the local market hall in order to support small, local merchants.

It is also well worth taking an *aluguer* (collective taxi) and head to Espargos or Palmeira. Here, you will still find plenty of small shops and bars managed by the local population.

8.2. SUSTAINABLE HOLIDAYS IN BOA VISTA

Boa Vista is the other tourist hub of the Cape Verdean archipelago. The vast beaches and immense dunes are attracting people from many European countries. Extremely well connected to major European airports, Boa Vista is one of the most popular places for Cape Verde winter holidays as well.

Larger than Sal, in Boa Vista you can still enjoy a certain sensation of emptiness and pristine state.

Most tourist resorts are located next to Sal Rei and managed by some of the largest hotel brands in the world. Walk the extra mile and you will stumble upon the legendary *morabeza*, the Cape Verdean hospitality!

WHERE TO STAY

Luckily, there are still plenty of smaller hotels in Boa Vista that are managed by local families. If you are looking for a warm welcome and learning about the Creole culture, staying at a smaller hotel is one of the best ways to do so. Spingueira Ecolodge *** is a pioneer when it comes to sustainable hotels in Boa Vista and has excellent reviews.

Estrela do Mar

Hotel Dunas ***

Terra Kriola

Pensão Santa Isabel

LOCAL SHOPS

There are two local markets in Sal Rei where you can buy handicrafts from Cape Verde and the West African coast.

There are plenty of souvenir shops selling items "Made in China", but the further you go from the sea, the more likely you will find the local merchants.

LOCAL RESTAURANTS

- *Wakan Bar*
- *Bar Bombli*
- *Blue Mery*
- *Porton di nos Ilha*

LOCAL GUIDES

Melitour (+2382511885)

Morabitur (+2389187309)

Morena (+2382511445)

Verdemundo (+2382512118)

Santo Antao attracts a very different type of travelers than Sal or Boa Vista. As the island has only very few beaches which are hard to access, mostly hikers and outdoor lovers visit Santo Antao.

As a result, there are not many large, international hotels. The local community manages most accommodation options. Surprisingly, there is a large number of eco-friendly hotels and lodges.

WHERE TO STAY

For hiking holidays in Santo Antao, I recommend staying either in Ribeira Grande or Ponta do Sol, as you will be close to the most important trails.

However, if you want to get a sense of remoteness and the extraordinary beauty of Santo Antao, then op for a few nights in the mountains.

If you want to include some days at the beach, head to Tarrafal. The access road is difficult but definitely worth it! There are several guesthouses to accommodate you.
>
> Biosfera Amor do dia
> Cantinho de Amizade
> Tiduca Hotel ****
> Divin Art
> CasaMaracuja – Aldeamento turistico Maracuja
> Sissi B&B (my home away for several weeks – the owner is the sweetest!)

LOCAL SHOPS IN SANTO ANTAO

- *Son & Art* (Porto Novo)
- *Loja de Artesanato* (Ribeira Grande)
- *Paul Natur* (Cidade das Pombas)
- *Cheese Factory* (Porto Novo)

LOCAL RESTAURANTS

- *Casa Maracuja* (one of my favorite places!)
- *Divin' Art*
- *Cantinho de Amizade*
- *Gato Preto*
- *Cozinha de Bento* (famous for their Durch apple pie and self-roasts coffee)

LOCAL GUIDES

Edson, my all-time favorite guide! - edsondal@live.com.pt

HOW TO SUPPORT THE LOCAL CULTURE

In any larger municipality of the island, you will find small, cute shops with souvenirs based on hand-made jams, *grogue* or liquor. However, increasingly, you will also stumble upon hand-made jewelry made from raw materials such as seeds or banana leaves.

One of my favorite places to enjoy the local culture is the *7sois7Luas* center in Ribeira Grande. It is the cultural hub of the island, where you can enjoy exhibitions, concerts and the local cuisine. It even has a cute shop where you can buy local goods.

8.4. SUSTAINABLE HOLIDAYS IN SAO VICENTE

To me, Sao Vicente has the evenest mix of beaches and hiking. There is the legendary Laginha Beach, Salamansa Bay, and the stunning Praia Grande of Calhau. Hiking lovers will find heaven there to hike up Monte Verde!

However, Sao Vicente, and more specifically Mindelo, are most famous for their cultural and musical scene! Home to the legendary singer *Cesaria Evora*, Mindelo is without any doubt one of the most bustling towns in Cape Verde. Plenty of music bars and local shops are awaiting you!

WHERE TO STAY

While there are several larger hotels in Mindelo, recently, many smaller, family-run businesses have opened their doors. It is thus a great occasion to support the local businesses!

If you are looking to escape the bustle of Mindelo, I recommend staying at Sao Pedro or Calhau Beach, which both boast a gorgeous bay.

> Simabo's Backpackers' Hostel (managed by an animal charity association)
> Aquiles Eco Hotel (Sao Pedro)
> Chez Loutcha Residencial (Mindelo)
> Pousada Montecara **** (Lazareto Monte Cara)
> Hotel Residencial GOA (Calhau)
> Terra Lodge (Mindelo)

LOCAL SHOPS

- *Lucy's* (Mindelo)
- *Trapos Polibel* (Mindelo)

- *Swell D'Sul* (Mindelo)
- CapVertDesign+Artesanato (Mindelo)
- Atelier Violao Aniceto Gomes (Mindelo)

LOCAL RESTAURANTS

- *Elvis Restobar* (Mindelo)
- *Chave d'Ouro* (Mindelo)
- *Pastelaria Morabeza* (Mindelo)
- *Dokas* (Mindelo)
- *Restaurante Hamburg* (Calhau)
- *Chez Loutcha* (Mindelo & Calhau)
- *Onda Morna Restaurante* (Mindelo)

LOCAL GUIDES

Cabetur (+2382323847)

Cibertur (+2382325610)

Djambai Tours (djambaitours@gmail.com)

8.5. SUSTAINABLE HOLIDAYS IN SANTIAGO

I compare a bit Santiago to Sao Vicente: plenty of cultures, gorgeous beaches, and hiking trails. However, the hiking trails of Serra Malagueta, in the heart of Santiago, are much more impressive! They really will give you the sensation of being away from the world.

Not to mention that you have Cidade Velha, one of the oldest, colonial towns that was once the main hub for the slave trade.

Santiago preserved its authentic flavour. It also boasts a gorgeous architecture in the "Plateau" district of Praia, and stunning nature.

WHERE TO STAY

For those who follow me a little longer, you know that I am a nature girl. I liked to spend a few nights in Praia just to get the feel of it and to indulge a bit in "western luxury".

However, it is in the interior of the island and in Tarrafal beach, in the north of the island where Santiago shows all its beauty.

Praia Baisco Big Lanche (Praia Baixo)
Pousada Praia Maria *** (Praia)
Syd's Guesthouse (Praia)
Pensão Asa Branca *** (Assomada)
Kama Ku Kafé – Pousada and B&B (Cidade Velha)
Vista Mar (Tarrafal)

LOCAL SHOPS

- *Associação de Artesãos da Ilha de Santiago* (Praia)
- *Bayela'Art* (Praia)
- *Art Gallery e Café* (Praia)
- *Lembrança di Terra* (Praia)

LOCAL RESTAURANTS

- *Kaza Katxupa* (Praia)
- *Tambake* (Praia, vegetarian restaurant!)
- *Casa da Sogra* (Praia)
- *Casa de Sonhos nos ilhas* (Praia)
- *TimeOut* (Assomada, in love with *Alice* the cook, and her food!)

LOCAL GUIDES

Barracuda Tours (Praia)

Novatur (Praia)

MultiviagensTour (Car Rental + Tours)

Praiatur (Praia, Santiago + tours to neighbor islands)

8.6. SUSTAINABLE CAPE VERDE HOLIDAYS IN FOGO

Fogo is unlike any other Cape Verdean island. With the colorful houses of its capital Sao Filipe, the austere village Chã das Caldeiras set in the volcano crater and the lush green coffee plantations near Mosteiros, Fogo is extremely diverse to say it with one word.

Whereas foreigners have opened plenty of new hotels and restaurants, you can still find some purely local businesses.

When it comes to hiking the volcano, make sure to go only with official guides. I strongly recommend contacting Alcindo from casa alcindo to organize your hike.

WHERE TO STAY

If you visit Fogo, you cannot leave without visiting Cha das Caldeiras. I would recommend spending two nights in Sao Filipe and a minimum of two nights in Cha das Caldeiras. Both villages are extremely laid-back but have their unique vibe.

Cha das Caldeiras is for me a place out of this world. Destroyed by the volcano eruption of 2015, the local community is slowly coming back and rebuilding their houses from scratch.

By staying overnight in Cha das Caldeiras, you are supporting their initiative of rebuilding their village. It is a marvelous place and it has the most incredible starry sky!

In Sao Filipe:

Hotel Residencial Savana ***
The Colonial Guest House
Casas do Sol ***
Casa Anilda & Albino

In Cha das Caldeiras:

Casa Alcindo
Casa Marisa 2.0
Ciza e Rose

LOCAL SHOPS

- Local market
- Local supermarkets (to stock up on the local Fogo vine, and organic coffee!)
- Souvenirs shops (souvenirs made with volcanic stone from Cha das Caldeiras!)
- *Dja'r Fogo* (artisan coffee from Fogo!)

LOCAL RESTAURANTS

- *Espaco 24*
- *Tropical Club*
- *Arko-Iris*
- *Me d'Rua*

In the crater:

- *Casa Alcindo* (delicious meals!)
- *Bar David Fernandes Montrond* (serving homemade *manekon* wine!)

LOCAL GUIDES

- *Alcindo* and his brothers (the official guides, contact *Casa Alcindo*)
- *Qualitur* (for round-the-island trips!)

8.7. SUSTAINABLE HOLIDAYS IN BRAVA

Brava is without any doubt one of the most remote islands of Cape Verde. That is first due to the ferry connections and the fact that there is no airport. Secondly, the sea to Brava can be very rough!

During centuries, it was difficult to reach the island. That is why Brava preserved a unique heritage and a very united community.

If you decide to visit Brava (and you definitely should!), you will get to experience the somehow pristine, unspoiled Cape Verde.

WHERE TO STAY

There are two main towns to stay when traveling to Brava. Nova Sintra, the enchanting capital and Fajã da Agua, famous for its gorgeous swimming pools.

Both towns are perfect departure points for long hikes that are the best way to explore the "island of flowers".

Djabraba's EcoLodge Giandinoto's Place
Hotel Cruz Grande-Brava ***
Residensia Ka Denxu

LOCAL SHOPS

The *7Sois7Luas* center in Nova Sintra has a beautiful shop with crafted items.

There are some shops in Nova Sintra selling traditional embroidery, cloth and lace dolls. In the villages, some artisans sell basketwork and stone carvings.

LOCAL RESTAURANTS

- *Bar Mansa* (+2382851222)
- *Hotel Djabraba's Eco-Lodge*
- *Esplanada Sodadi*
- *Pôr-do-Sol* (Faja d'Agua)
- Ponto de Encontro (+2382851623)

LOCAL GUIDES

Qualitur

Ask for a local guide at the *7Sois7Luas* center

HOW TO SUPPORT THE LOCAL CULTURE

Brava is also one of the islands that has one of the most important rates of emigration towards the USA. Thus, your visit and decision to support the local businesses will give the people a reason to continue investing in this pristine island.

I also recommend getting in touch with the cultural association of 7Sois7Luas who supports guides and organizes concerts on a regular basis.

8.8. SUSTAINABLE HOLIDAYS IN MAIO

There are three beach islands in Cape Verde. Two of them, Sal and Boa Vista have been "spoiled" by mass tourism. Luckily, you still have Maio! In my opinion, Maio is just on the edge of becoming a new tourist destination. Thus, there are still plenty of options to support local, small businesses!

Maio is synonymous with virgin beaches where you will not cross anybody for hours! To me, it is home to the best beaches in Cape Verde! It is synonymous with a friendly, peaceful community and nature in its pristine state.

A gem that will learn hopefully from the errors committed in Sal and Boa Vista when it comes to tourism.

WHERE TO STAY IN MAIO FOR SUSTAINABLE HOLIDAYS

Most accommodation sites are in Vila do Maio, also known as "Porto Ingles". However, if you are looking for absolute peace and tranquillity, head to Morro or Calheta where you will have vast beaches all for your own!

If most of the recommended places here are not on Booking, it is simply because of the unawareness or the lack of funds to pay a high commission.

> Villa Maris Ecolodge (Morro)
>
> Residencial BON SOSSEGO Bar Restaurante
>
> Pensão Casa Sousa
>
> Residencial Porto Ingles (+2382551698)

LOCAL SHOPS

- *Info Artesanato* (Main Esplanade, Porto Ingles)
- *Cheese Factory* (Ribeira Dom Joao)
- *Salinas Museum Shop*
- Senegalese Tailor (behind the *7Sois7Luas* center)

LOCAL RESTAURANTS

- *7Sois7Luas* (best views on the beach!)
- *Bar Tibau* (managed by the legendary singer *Tibau Tavares!*, Main Avenue, Porto Ingles)
- *Bar Tropikal* (Beach Porto Ingles)
- *Contina* (homemade, Cape Verdean food for 4 €!)
- *Horace Silver Lounge Bar* (best cocktails in town!)
- *Mar i Sol* (behind the *7Sois7Luas* restaurant, best-fried *moreira* (eel) in town!)
- *Bar Garage* (near the post office, for coffee and homemade yogurts!)

LOCAL GUIDES

Bemvindo (+2389959713)

Contina Viagens (+2389874866)

Maio Biodiversity Foundation (for eco-tours!)

HOW TO SUPPORT THE LOCAL CULTURE

The best way to support the local culture and sustainable tourism in Maio is by staying and eating out at the local businesses.

It is not that I have anything about hotels or restaurants managed by foreigners! I am just deeply convinced that also, if not mostly, the local population should have its share from the benefits of the growing tourism industry!

Yes, eating out or staying at a Cape Verdean hotel is different from a European hotel! Then still, what is the purpose of traveling when you want the same things than back at home? Thus, give local businesses a chance to see that it is worth investing in tourism and give them the hope to be able to grow!

During the week, Maio is relatively quiet. However, during the weekends, you can enjoy plenty of live music in *7Sois7Luas*, *Horace Silver Lounge Bar* or in *Bar Tropikal*.

9. HELPFUL EXPRESSIONS IN CAPE VERDEAN CREOLE

The Cape Verdeans speak Creole but consider Portuguese as their second language. Depending on the island, English is widely spoken as well. However, if you want to make real connections with the locals or simply come closer to the Cape Verdean vibe, I can only recommend bearing the following expressions (in Creole!) in mind.

Please note that these phrases in Creole (Kriol, Creolle, or Criollo) can vary a lot throughout the islands! There is a Cape Verdean Creole for the Northern Islands and one of the Southern Islands

1. TUD DRET?

When you walk in the streets of Mindelo or on the windy roads of Santo Antao, people will ask you all the time: *"Tud dret?"* It generally comes with a thumbs-up move and a big positive smile.

It can be freely translated by "Everything all right?" and is used in all kind of situations. I ended up asking *"Tud dret?"* to almost everybody I crossed in the street! Just like most Cape Verdeans do.

A variation of *"Tud dret?"* is *"Tud fixe?"* (Pronounced *"Tud fiche"*)

2. SAB P'AFRONTA!

This is the best answer that you can give to *"Tud dret?"* "*Sap!*" in creole means "Cool!" If you are being asked your opinion on something or just asked how you are feeling, "*Sap!*" is the most authentic way to answer.

"Sap pa fronte!" is the comparison of "*Sap!*" and lets everybody know that you are feeling fabulous. Alternatively, that you like something very much.

I used *"Sap pa fronte!"* almost every day. Either when I was asked how I was doing or if I was enjoying Cape Verde. *"Sap pa fronte!"* "Of course, I did!"

Please note that this expression is mostly used in Sal, Sao Vicente and Santo Antao.

3. SEBIM

Food plays a very important role in Cape Verde! Especially when it comes to *bafas* (the Cape Verdean version of *tapas*), the matter is very serious! Most *bafas* come from the sea: *moreia* (fried moray), *buzios* (shell entrails), *lapas* (limpets), cod croquettes, etc.

Each more delicious than the other and the perfect match to your cold beer!

If the waiter asks you if you are enjoying your meal, a determined "*Sebim!*" is the best way to answer! It can be freely translated by "It tastes good!"

It is always good to know how to make a cook happy! Especially in his own language!

In the Southern Islands, "*Sebim!*" becomes often "*Sabim!*"

---

4. CACHUPA

Let us stick to the food (my favorite topic!). For those who love to travel culinary (like me!), *cachupa* is a "must-try" when you visit Cape Verde! The national dish of the archipelago can be eaten for breakfast, lunch or dinner. Anytime is *cachupa* time!

Cachupa needs to be cooked for several hours on an open fire. Some say that is the reason why on several islands, almost no trees are left! Hearty food lovers will enjoy it! The stew consists of corn, beans, and sweet potato slices. Optionally, tuna or pork meat can be added.

It is usually served with a fried egg on top and a *linguiça* (spicy sausage). *Cachupa* is normally the cheapest dish on the menu and keeps you satiated during hours!

"*Sebim!* ", "It tastes great!"

---

5. ALUGUER

In Cape Verde, you do not catch a bus to get to your destination, but you get there by *aluguer* or *colectivo*. *Aluguers* usually consist of vans with up to 15 seats..., which does not necessarily limit them to 15 people...!

Apparently, the Cape Verdeans love to travel "closely together". Do not be surprised if you will be asked to take a kid on your lap.

Aluguers do not run according to a schedule. They depart when nobody else can fit in (literally!). Since waiting for the last person to fit in can take up to one hour, you had better choose an *aluguer* that is already mostly fully charged.

Drivers will sometimes ask you if you want to get to your destination by "taxi". This means that you will travel alone in the van but the price will increase tenfold (not exaggerating!). If you prefer the more economical version, just insist on traveling by *aluguer* or *colectivo*. In addition, oh magic; the price decreases!

In the Southern Islands, a *colectivo* is also known as "*yas*".

6. PONCHE & GROGUE

You cannot leave Cape Verde without having tried its national drinks: *grogue* and *ponche*! *Grogue* is made out of distilled sugar cane and can have up to 40% of alcohol!

Grogue is the basis of *ponche* including molasses, lime, and fruit. *Ponche* can be compared to liqueur and is much sweeter than *grogue*.

Some say that *grogue* can heal you from every evil! Be that a headache or a cold! They cannot be so wrong about it since, after one *grogue* shot, you truely feel "disinfected" inside out! I loved to have *grogue* in my *caipirinha*.

Conversely, *ponche* is a real sweet treat! There are many kinds: coconut, honey, passion fruit (my favorite!) or tamarind. Just try them all and find your own favorite!

7. MORNA

Cape Verde rhymes with music! You can hear music everywhere in the streets of Mindelo or in Sal. The archipelago's most famous music style is called "*morna*". *Cesaria Evora* (worshiped as a goddess, especially in Mindelo!), exported *morna* to the world. On the anniversary of her death, her family organizes a commemoration march through Mindelo and a concert in her honor.

The stage is set right next to the entrance of her former house and the A-list of Cape Verdean artists is performing.

Morna is all about *sodade*, a melancholic feeling of nostalgia. In this way, *morna* can be compared to the Portuguese *fado*. In

Mindelo, you can listen to *morna* in almost every bar, but I recommend *Casa da Morna* and *Livraria Nho Djunga* to attend live concerts.

8. MORABEZA

Morabeza refers to the Cape Verdean concept of hospitality and the kindness of its people. The term is synonymous to their relaxed and gentle way to welcome strangers on the archipelago.

I felt the *morabeza* the most when I was on Santo Antao. This place became one of my favorite spots on this planet!

People welcome you with a bright smile and they transfer you a bit of their relaxed composure.

Everybody greets you on the street ("*Tud dret?* ") and some even offered me their houses to stay, or gave me to taste ripe fruits of their gardens.

I felt very fortunate to experience the ominous *morabeza* first-hand! It made me feel like at home and it was the reason why I prolonged my stay twice!

9. ORIL GAME

If you wander through the streets of Sao Filipe (Fogo) or Porto Ingles (Maio), you will always stumble upon a group of people playing the popular *Oril* game. You will find them in bars or sitting on a bench in front of their house.

You will immediately recognize this strategic game as the board consists of a wooden trunk with 12 openings. Each player has 24 green, small balls, called "olives" that have to be placed strategically in the wooden openings.

The game comes from the west coast of Africa and was brought to Cape Verde by the slaves during Portuguese colonialism.

10.   LOCAL FOOD GUIDE

A former colony of Portugal until 1975, Cape Verde has known how to blend its West African heritage with European influences.

It is a great place for adventurers and beachgoers, but also for foodies looking to discover a unique cuisine.

Like everything else, the Cape Verdean food showcases Portuguese and West African influences.

This rich blend of culture gave birth to unique gastronomy. The Creole society has further shaped the Cape Verdean cuisine. Here, you can expect explosions of flavors and aromas that will surprise even well-versed chefs.

If it is true that tasting local food is essential for fully understanding a culture, then you definitely have to try these Cape Verdean dishes during your stay or read the recipes to prepare them at home.

10.1. CACHUPA

A staple of Cape Verdean culture, *cachupa* is more than just a national dish. Proudly prepared by locals for the most various occasions, this hearty stew can easily be defined as the Cape Verdean comfort food par excellence.

Born as "food for the poor", *cachupa* can surprise your taste buds in many different ways. Nowadays, most restaurants, propose the cachupa "rica" (the "rich" version), prepared with various meats and sometimes even tuna.

The *cachupa* "pobre" (the "poor" version) is still the one you can taste in most homes. Locals prepare it with pork fat, rather than meat, in order to keep the costs low.

No matter what variant you decide to prepare, *cachupa refogada* makes up for an exquisite lunch. This variety of *cachupa* is made from either *rica* or *pobre* leftovers and is usually served with fried eggs and sausages.

The Cape Verdean *cachupa* is time-consuming to prepare. Traditionally, it's made on Saturdays, and many restaurants around the islands only serve it once a week. But if you don't get a chance to taste it while in Cape Verde, here is an easy recipe to try at home.

If you like fish and seafood more than meat, then *buzio* is definitely a dish to try in Cape Verde.

This slow-cooked food is typically made with mussels (although other shellfish can also be used), and soy sauce.

Not as hearty as the Cape Verdean *cachupa, buzio* is a better choice for a lighter lunch or dinner, as well as for a festive meal.

10.3.   MORREIA - FRIED MORAY EEL

Morreia (fried moray eel) is one of those dishes that stand as proof of the strong Portuguese influences the Cape Verdean culture had over the decades.

A staple of the Portuguese cuisine, *Morreia* is one of the most popular dishes in Cape Verde too.

The secret here is to briefly brine the eel, then cut it in small portions and fry it until crispy.

On the menu in most restaurants and bars in Cape Verde, the fried eel is ideal for lunch or dinner and also a delicious snack to enjoy with cocktails.

Having *Morreia frita* with friends during a warm summer night is definitely one of the best things to do in Cape Verde.

While its name might remind of the Maghrebi couscous, the Cape Verdean *Bol de Cus-Cus* is an entirely different dish. It's usually served for breakfast and ideal for anyone with a sweet tooth.

Made with cornmeal, sugar, and cinnamon, this is the type of food you either love or hate.

Regardless of the outcome though, this is definitely a dish to try if you want to immerse yourself completely into the culture of the Cape Verde islands.

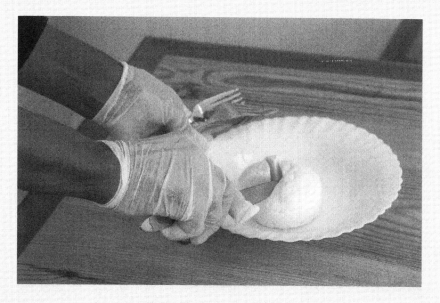

Who doesn't love cheese? It is a staple all over the world, and Cape Verde has its famous cheese too. On its islands, goat cheese is not only appreciated by locals, but it's also a true delight for its visitors.

This type of fresh cheese has a soft, silky texture, fine taste, and creamy consistency. The best is produced by farmers in the small villages located high up the mountains of Santo Antão, as well as on Fogo, but you can easily find it all over Cape Verde.

Thanks to its delicate flavor, the Cape Verdean goat cheese is perfect for both sweet and savoury dishes. Locals usually pair it with papaya marmalade.

You could also enjoy their tasty cheese pudding, a delicious dessert praised by Cape Verdeans and tourists alike.

In Cape Verde, seafood lovers are undoubtedly spoilt with choices. From lobster to shellfish, there are quite a few options to choose from.

One of them is *percebes*, a small crustacean that lives in colonies on the seabed rocks.

Despite their rather peculiar look, *percebes* are absolutely delicious. According to the Portuguese tradition, they are often served with buttered toast and pair wonderfully with a glass of draft beer or a *grogue*, the national Cape Verdean spirit.

For an authentic experience, you must try this dish in one of the many beach bars or terraces that dot the coastal landscape of all islands.

Food in Cape Verde is often based on so-called "poor" ingredients, but this doesn't mean it's not tasty.

If you're a soup or stew lover, *jagacida* is an unmissable dish to try. Like *cachupa*, *jagacida* has many regional varieties, but in essence, it's a Portuguese-style rice and beans stew.

Depending on what you like to put in it, *jagacida* makes for a great lunch or dinner. It can be served as a side for sausages or grilled octopus.

No matter how you serve it, rest assured you'll be impressed by this authentic Cape Verdean recipe. It's a must when looking for traditional Cape Verdean food.

One thing you'll find out quickly when visiting Cape Verde is that there are so many fish or seafood Cape Verdean recipes that you'll be spoiled with choices when ordering your lunch or dinner.

Besides the fried eel I already mentioned, Cape Verde is mostly famous for its delicious tuna cooked in a variety of ways. This fish is so delicious that some even prepare the traditional "rich" *cachupa* with tuna steaks instead of meat.

Bonito, serra as well as *esmoregal* are served in many eateries across Cape Verde, while octopus and groupers cooked in a variety of ways are served both as appetizers or mains.

Cape Verde is also popular for its spider crabs and *buzio*, a "rubbery"+ shellfish that's a regular on most plates.

While fish can be cooked in many ways, one of the best Cape Verdean food recipes you must try is *caldo de peixe*, a traditional fish soup. It's a typical Cape Verdean soup that is particularly popular in Sao Vicente.

10.9.   XERÉM

Xerém is another Cape Verde food derived from the country's Portuguese heritage. It is popular in Portugal, Cape Verde, and Brazil. However, each country has a traditional recipe that makes it unique.

In Cabo Verde, Xerém is more or less the savory alternative to the sweet cus-cus. It is prepared from corn wheat mixed with water, butter, salt, and bay leaves.

While you can taste many regional varieties, the most popular is Xerém de festa, a festive dish prepared with pork, fat, onions, beans, bay leaves, spices, and tomatoes.

Most restaurants serve it at least once a week. If you're after an authentic Cape Verdean experience, you should taste XERÉM during the drum festival on the island of Brava, one of the most beautiful Cape Verde islands.

10.10. FRANGO ASSADO - GRILLED CHICKEN

There is nothing quite like enjoying a nice spicy chicken after soaking up the sun for the whole day. After all, the West African *peri peri* grilled chicken is famous throughout the world for a reason.

While this amazing dish can surely lift you up on a cold winter day, it can also restore your energy levels and get you ready for a night out in Cape Verde.

Known as *frango assado*, Cape Verde's grilled chicken is really delicious.

Obviously, what makes it special is the traditional *peri peri* spice.

So, if you like your food a little spicier, you surely have to taste the original, while exploring your favourite Cape Verdean Island.

10.11. LAPAS -LIMPETS

I can't emphasize enough how many exquisite seafood dishes Cape Verde has, and among them, one you have to try is *lapas*.

It is the Portuguese name for limpet, a species of shellfish that is usually grilled and served with garlic and butter.

Hardcore seafood lovers may also appreciate it raw, with a squeeze of lemon juice on top. You can even find *lapas* in some fish soups and stews.

If there is one thing the Cape Verdean people can brilliantly do, it's to merge the West African flavors with the Portuguese ones in tasty combinations.

The Cape Verdean *pastel* is one of the most popular fusion recipes, and definitely a food you must try while visiting the islands. It is often sold in small streets of larger towns in Maio, Fogo, and Brava.

Unlike the famous *pastel de nata* (the famous Portuguese dessert), the pastels in Cape Verde are more similar to the Argentinian *empanadas* a savory delight.

Often called *pastel com diablo dentro* ("*pastel* with the devil inside"), this spicy food is typically made with tuna fish, garlic and chili.

The filling doesn't necessarily have to be hot and you can find all kinds of fish *pastels* in restaurants or also in food stalls in the local markets.

If you don't really like tuna, know that this devilishly tasty *pastels* can also be prepared with white fish (usually sea bream or halibut), while some even propose varieties with meat.

10.13. KAVALA

While the official Cape Verde language is Portuguese, most locals speak Cape Verdean creole. And something you'll hear the street vendors scream in this beautiful dialect is "*kavala fresk*" ("fresh KAVALA").

In Creole, *kavala* means mackerel, but it's also the name of a dish made with rice and fish.

Not only is this one of the most popular Cape Verdean foods, but an annual festival is also held in June or July to celebrate mackerel in all its forms.

10.14. TYPICAL FRUITS FROM CAPE VERDE

Besides its delicious dishes, Cape Verde is also popular for its exquisite fresh fruits.

All it takes is a stroll through one of the colorful markets on the main islands to find an abundant offer of mangoes, bananas, coconuts, avocado and other tropical fruits you can eat as a snack or dessert.

10.15. PUDIM DE LEITE - MILK PUDDING

Moving on from savory to sweet dishes, know that there are many Cape Verde recipes that can satisfy your sweet tooth. The *pudim de leite* is one of the most popular sweets in Cape Verde.

Similar to the Spanish flan, this milk pudding topped with caramel can melt even the toughest hearts.

10.16. DOCE DE COCO - COCONUT CANDY

Doce de coco is a Cape Verde traditional food you have to try while visiting the islands. This simple sweet is made with butter, sugar, and coco, and cooked for hours until it transforms into tasty chunks.

Not only most restaurants serve it, but you can also find it at street food stalls.

Eating delicious food is only part of an exquisite lunch or dinner. Drinks matter too, and Cape Verde spoils you with choices. The traditional drink here is *grogue*, a type of spirit distilled from sugar canes and very similar to rum.

Due to the artisanal production, there are various *grogue* qualities on the market. If you aim to taste the best, head to Santiago or Santo Antao.

Ponche is the traditional Cape Verdean cocktail, made with *grogue*, lime, and molasses. Somewhat similar to a *mojito* but sweeter, this is undeniably a drink to try in Cape Verde.

10.18. WINE FROM FOGO

Africa has a strong presence on the world's wine map, and some of the best wine in West Africa comes from Cape Verde.

Produced in the small village of CHA DAS CALDEIRAS on Fogo, the Cape Verdean wine is praised for its superior quality.

A unique terroir (constituted by volcanic soils) and a perfect microclimate create the perfect conditions for the proper development of the vines.

The grapes here have high sugar content, an essential requisite for the production of high-quality dry or sweet red, rosé, and white wines.

10.19. CAIPIRINHAS CAPE VERDEAN STYLE

Last but not least, drinking a good cocktail is a must while visiting Cape Verde. *Ponche* apart, the islands are also known for their CAIPIRINHAS.

Like the Brazilian ones, CAIPIRINHAS here come in all styles, made with either lemon, passion fruit, pineapple or other tropical fruits.

The main difference between the Cape Verdean CAIPIRINHAS and all others is the use of *grogue* as spirit. Thus, you can expect a unique burst of flavors you won't be able to find elsewhere.

10.20. CALABACEIRA - BAOBAB JUICE

When looking for traditional drinks from Cape Verde, you can't skip *Calabaceira*, Baobab juice! You can drink it at almost every bar or restaurant in the country.

If you don't add too much sugar to it, Babobab juice is one of the healthiest drinks out there. Indeed, it comes with plenty of Vitamin C (more than an orange), minerals and natural fibre.

The good thing is that it is very easy to make at home. It took me less than 30 min. All you need is Baobab powder and water.

10.21. BISSAP - HIBISCUS JUICE

One of my favorite drinks from Cape Verde is without any doubt "*bissap*", hibiscus juice. On hot days, it's extremely refreshing.

It's a typical drink from West African countries, but you can also find it in Caribbean or Asian countries. I loved the diversity of recipes!

You can find *bissap* juice in almost every bar in Cape Verde. It's often served with sugar but you can always request that you want it served without sugar.

Another reason why I love hibiscus juice from Cabo Verde so much are its almost infinite health benefits. It's jam-packed with antioxidants and it was also found that consuming hibiscus tea lowered blood pressure in people at risk of high blood pressure.

You can serve hibiscus juice hot or iced.

It's super easy to make! All you need is water and dried hibiscus flowers.

FREE RESOURCES

Free printables:

- Cape Verde travel packing list
- Printable bucket list

Recommended apps:

- Wise – for cash withdrawal and safe card payments. When signing up you get a free card.
- Maps.me – offline maps and hiking trails
- Komoot – hiking trails
- Wikiloc – hiking trails
- Divisa plus – currency conversion

Online resources:

- Trivago – Best hotel deals
- Skyscanner – best flight deals
- CV Interilhas – Ferries between islands
- Bestfly – flights between islands
- Viator – tours and activities
- iVisa – book visa online in advance
- HeyMondo – travel and health insurance
- Souvenirs – list with Cape Verde-themed gifts

OBRIGADA!

Thank you so much for reading and I really hope that you enjoyed this guide book.

Do you have any suggestions or tips how I could improve this book? Or did you make a discovery in Cape Verde that you absolutely find worth to be mentioned in this travel guide? Feel free to shoot me a message on info(a)paulinaontheroad.com

I can't wait to hear from you!

Happy travels!

Paulina

Printed in Great Britain
by Amazon

18492864R00165